National 5 English

Reading for Understanding, Analysis and Evaluation

Introduction

Your parents may have known it as *Interpretation*. In primary school it's often called *Comprehension*. Up until recently, it was labelled *Close Reading*. At the moment, it is referred to as *Reading for Understand, Analysis, and Evaluation*. Whatever the SQA (Scottish Qualifications Authority) wish to call this skill, the process is pretty simple: read a passage, usually from a newspaper, and answer a series of questions.

Simple. Right?

Well, actually, the process can be a lot more difficult in practice. For starters, many of the passages are quite tricky to comprehend. There are complex lines-of-thought and challenging vocabulary and references which, if you're not widely read, are often missed or misunderstood. Then there are the different question types – word choice, sentence structure, link, and imagery, just to name a few. Finally, there are the expected responses. In order to gain full marks, a pupil's answers need to be detailed and insightful. A good answer should "unpick" and "tease out" the meaning of the language used. When discussing ideas, a pupil needs to have the vocabulary in order to translate key points into their own words. All of this can often leave pupils feeling intimidated by this section of the exam.

As experienced teachers, we know that practice papers are invaluable when preparing for exams. This book starts out with brief explanations about how to answer each of the different question types which typically appear on the Reading for Understand, Analysis and Evaluation portion of the National 5 English exam. The bulk of this textbook is comprised of a series of practice papers. Working though each practice paper and, most importantly, comparing their response to the detailed marks schemes provided, will help pupils improve their ability to successfully answer the different question types.

While Reading for Understanding, Analysis, and Evaluation can be demanding, with practice, pupils can make real progress.

We wish you every success with your National 5 English exam.

Tom Smart
&
James Getty

Question Types

As the name would suggest, *Reading for Understanding, Analysis and Evaluation* is comprised of three main question types: Understanding, Analysis, and Evaluation. Each question type focuses on a different aspect of a passage / text. The question types can be summarised as follows:

- **Understanding** – this question type focuses on key ideas of the passage and asks pupils to explain the content of a passage
- **Analysis** – this question type focuses on the language of the passage and asks pupils to explain language techniques used in the passage
- **Evaluation** – this question type focuses on pupils' reactions or opinions to a passage and asks them if they found the passage successful or unsuccessful, supported by evidence from the text

Understanding Question Types

Understanding questions can be broken down into roughly five subcategories:

- Own Words
- Summary
- Explain
- Link
- Context

On the surface, understanding questions are quite simple. For example, pupils might be asked to put a portion of a text into their own words. Seems easy enough, a pupil might think: find the bit of the passage I need, and then change the words. However, in order to be able to complete this seemingly straightforward task, a pupil must first be able to comprehend what they have read. This means that they need to have the vocabulary to access a passage, the contextual knowledge for key ideas to make sense, and the language skills to translate complex thoughts into their own words. Suddenly, an own words question is not so easy.

The following formulas and tips will help pupils to answer the different understanding question types. Pupils should be aware that the formulas given are only guidelines, and there is often more than one correct way to answer each question type.

Question Type / Tips	Formula / Process
<u>Own Words</u> *In your own words, what is the author's opinion in lines...* Pupils should NOT quote from the passage. If a question is worth two marks, then pupils should provide two pieces of information. When a question is worth three marks, then three pieces of information should be provided, etc. Finally, pupils must make certain that they refer to the exact part of the passage which the question specifies.	• Isolate the relevant part of the passage • Change key words • Check the number of marks
<u>Explain</u> *Explain the author's key ideas in lines...* This question type is exactly the same as an own words question. Pupils should follow the same guidelines.	• Isolate the relevant part of the passage • Change key words • Check the number of marks
<u>Summarise</u> *Summarise the author's reasons in lines...* This question type is exactly the same as an own words question. Pupils should follow the same guidelines.	• Isolate the relevant part of the passage • Change key words • Check the number of marks
<u>Link</u> *How does the sentence in lines... act as a link in the author's argument...* Pupils must identify how a sentence in the passage connects key ideas. Linking language is typically found at the start of a paragraph or the end of a paragraph.	• <u>Quote</u> from the portion of the sentence which <u>links back</u> in the passage • Explain the key ideas contained in the quote and how they link back • <u>Quote</u> from the portion of the sentence which <u>links forward</u> in the passage • Explain the key ideas contained in the quote and how they link forward

Question Type / Tips	Formula / Process
Context *How does the context of lines... help to make the meaning of the word clear...* This question type asks pupil about the meaning of a word and how the surrounding texts helps to make the meaning of that word clear.	• Quote the word identified in the question • Define the word • Explain how the context (surrounding words) helped you to arrive at the meaning of the word or helped to make the meaning of the word clear

Analysis Question Types

Analysis question can be broken down into roughly four subcategories:

- Word Choice
- Imagery
- Sentence Structure
- Tone

In some respects, analysis questions are fairly clear-cut. Analysis questions are obsessed with technique – more specifically, how and why an author uses technique. Once a pupil is able to find the relevant technique, then all they need to do is to explain its effect. The problem with analysis questions is that the marks scheme can often be frustratingly pedantic for these question types. For word choice question pupils must remember to state what the word suggest, for imagery question pupils must explain the literal root of the image, for sentence structure questions pupils must specifically state what certain types of punctuation achieve… the list goes on.

In short, once pupils locate a language technique, they must stick to the proscribed formula. This will make certain that they don't omit key information.

Question Type / Tips	Formula / Process
Word Choice *How does the author's word choice help to make clear that…* Typically, pupils should only quote one word – occasionally, pupils could quote two words if, for clarity, it was necessary. In most cases, there is more than one word which will successfully answer the question. Pupils should try to choose the word they find easiest to explain.	• Quote a word • Give the connotations of the word (what the word suggests) • Explain why the author choose to use this word and how it emphasizes the author's viewpoint / ideas

Imagery *How does the author's use of imagery help to highlight their opinion…* Usually, imagery will focus on either simile or metaphor. More seldom, the question will ask about personification. The language "Just as" and "So too" can be helpful when explaining the commonalities of imagery. For example, in the metaphor: The man was a lion in battle. "Just as a lion is brave, so too was the man."	• Quote the simile or metaphor • Identify the comparison being made • In detail, explain the nature of the comparison / explain the commonality • Summarise why the author has chosen to use the simile or metaphor – how does it help to highlight their viewpoint / ideas
Sentence Structure *How does the author's use of sentence structure help to make clear that…* Pupils should be aware that there is a variety of ways in which an author might vary their sentence structure. For example: • Long Sentence / Short Sentence • Repetition • List • Punctuation – colon, semi-colon, quotation marks, dash, brackets • Rhetorical question • Parenthesis • Inversion • Climax / Anti-climax	• Quote the example of sentence structure • Identify the sentence structure used • Explain why the author has used this particular type of sentence structure and how it helps to emphasize their opinions / ideas
Tone There are several tones which pupils may come across For example: • Sarcastic • Critical • Optimistic • Negative	• State the author's tone • Explain how this tone is created and provide evidence (quote) from the text Note: Tone is often created through an author's word choice or arrangement of ideas.

Evaluation Questions

Generally, evaluation questions ask pupils whether they found an aspect of a passage successful or unsuccessful. These questions can ask about any aspect of the passage, but tend to focus on the opening paragraph or final paragraph of a passage. The majority of questions on an exam fall into the understanding or analysis question types, so evaluation questions can sometimes confuse pupils.

It is usually far easier to say that a passage has been successful. Typically, examination papers are drawn from newspapers, so the quality of the writing is to a good standard. In order to answer these types of questions, pupil must provide evidence for their opinion. This should take the form of a quotation with an explanation.

Question Type / Tips	**Formula / Process**
How effective do you find the final paragraph as a conclusion to the passage as a whole... **Evaluation** When providing evidence for whether the author has been successful, pupils may refer to either content (ideas) or language (techniques).	• State whether the passage has been successful or unsuccessful (in terms of quality of writing or ideas) • Quote evidence from the passage which supports your viewpoint • Explain, referencing either ideas or techniques, as to why this makes the passage successful or unsuccessful

Practice Papers

Table of Contents

War Comes to the Cinema

In this passage the author reflects on the first time he saw the film, "Saving Private Ryan", and how it changed his view of all war films.

It was a cold, rainy afternoon in 1998 when I went to see Steven Spielberg's "Saving Private Ryan". At that point I had an idea of what a war film was: in my war films the good guys won and the bad guys were killed because they deserved it. If a good guy died, the audience sighed as he made a touching final speech. Movies were all about some kind of justice in front of a camera, without a court room or a judge.

Steven Spielberg changed all of that by recreating on film something of what really happened in a war at 6.30am on the morning of June 6th, 1944. The code name for the time of the landing, everything was in code to create secrecy, was "H-hour". Squads of servicemen, usually thirty two to a landing craft, would leave their mother ship out in the channel. Their pilot would land them on the beach and return to the ship for more soldiers – the idea was that a fresh wave of troops would set foot on the beach every thirty minutes. Over thirty thousand were to be put ashore in the space of a few days. The military leaders thought that they would simply overpower and capture defenders who had run out of ammunition anyway. On Omaha beach, a five mile stretch of sand in Normandy, very little of this would go to plan.

Twenty-nine Sherman tanks were assigned to this area but only two made it ashore. The others became bogged down in the water with their trapped crews struggling to survive. Apart from their firepower, the tanks might have given the ordinary soldier, usually an easy target for German gunners, a little cover. In his film, Spielberg does not place a single tank on the sand, perhaps to underline to us just how vulnerable these young soldiers were. Of course, the planning for all of this had been intricate, but once the first shot is fired, military plans tend to evaporate in a chorus of fear and panic.

On the German side, rushed activity started at around 5am. Lookouts had spotted large ships off the coast and everybody would have been manning the guns. On the coast line at Vierville-sur-mer and elsewhere, more than eighty machine guns pointed out from their bunkers and trenches like alert blood hounds. Whoever landed on the beach would be their victim. In addition, the area was mined and the beach covered in steel obstacles, nicknamed "hedgehogs" to stop free movement. Who can know what went through the minds of the soldiers in the landing craft that morning? It was a mercy that they did not know then what the history books say now. General Omar Bradley, one of their commanders, had told them, no doubt with their morale in mind, that the naval bombardment which was to come before the landings, would weaken and discourage the German defenders. In truth the bombardment had little effect. For example, 12,000 German soldiers from the 352nd infantry division, half of them already experienced troops, stayed right where they were. They were ready, releasing the safety catches from their weapons, prepared to aim at their targets and fire.

In the film Captain Miller (played by Tom Hanks) tells his men in the landing craft that he will "see" them "on the beach", reminding them to keep the sand out of their weapons. In reality, he only sees a few of them again. As the protective door at the front of the craft is lowered, machine gun bullets, like water from a fire fighter's hose, kill many of them immediately. Although stomach churning, this is hardly a surprise. The MG42 gun the Germans had, built by the company Grossfuss Johannes, could fire up to 1,800 bullets a minute. It was the Rolls Royce of machine guns. In the film, Captain Miller sees only death and carnage on the beach. The shock of it all makes him hesitate in a trauma. He's not like the good guys in my films: the first soldier he tries to help is immediately shot through the heart. Desperately, he helps a second man, dragging him to safety, only to realise the man is already dead, cut in half by an explosion. At this point, I simply forgot this was a film. Bullets seem to fly past the camera lens; soldiers' uniforms puff up and tear as they fall in the sand. The only question running through my mind was: how do they do that?

Perhaps too graphic for the film would have been the plight of immobile, injured soldiers lying in the shallow water and then drowning as the tide came in. Horrible and disturbing enough, however, are the scenes where soldiers are riddled with bullets before their brand new boots touch the sand. It is their blood that turns the bright blue of the water into horror-movie red. The camera pans along the shore and shows you a few of them; on June 6th, 1944, almost two and a half thousand soldiers would be killed or injured. Somebody had to remove those bodies from the beach, making sure to note the service number on their "dog tag" identity necklace. Sixty days later Mr and Mrs Smith from Nebraska, or Mr and Mrs Jones from Rhode Island, would have received a letter, delivered conventionally in the mail, telling them their son had been killed in action. Unlike the film, the awful news would not be brought to them by a commanding officer or a sympathetic priest. The gap in time - sixty days- is explained with the fact that the exact location in France and the numbers killed or injured was still a secret. For many families, the reality was that their son was already dead before they even read about the invasion in the newspaper.

In "Saving Private Ryan", the justice I once liked in my war films was no longer in front of me. In one scene that clings to my memory like a tattoo, an injured man on the sand has his bleeding stopped by a group of medics, only to be shot cruelly in the head by a sniper. Even if you are wounded and vulnerable, the German guns have no mercy. However, neither side plays fair. When hardened American soldiers overrun the German trenches, they needlessly and brutally shoot surrendering Germans. On the beach, everyone is an easy target. The good guys against the bad guys format is destroyed. Spielberg makes sure of that.

Coming out of a Glasgow cinema into a cold, rainy evening, any discomfort the weather brought seemed trivial. Over half a century before me, soldiers on a beach once had far greater struggles. My concept of war films was nonsense, I realised. This film re-created the reality of warfare. Once you see it, you cannot forget it.

James Getty

Questions – War Comes to the Cinema

1. Look at lines 1 – 5.

   a. Using your **own words** as far as possible, what was the writer's idea of a war? (2 marks)

   b. How does the author's **word choice** help to emphasize his view of war films? (2 marks)

2. How does the **sentence structure** in lines 7 – 8 help to emphasize that the American and British troops did not want the Germans to know they were invading? (2 marks)

3. How does the writer's **word choice** in lines 16 – 22 convey to the reader what the soldiers' experience on the beach would have been like.

   You should use at least two examples in your answer. (4 marks)

4. How does the writer's **imagery** in lines 24 – 26 convey that the Germans were ready to fight? (2 marks)

5. Explain how the **sentence structure** in lines 30 – 33 help reveal General Omar Bradley's hope for the invasion. (2 marks)

6. In lines 38 – 42, how does **imagery** convey just how powerful the guns were? (2 marks)

7. Looking at lines 45 – 48, the writer forgets he is watching a film. Using your **own words** as far as possible, explain why this is so. (2 marks)

8. How does the sentence in lines 49 – 50 act as a link in this passage? (2 mark)

9. Referring to lines 55 – 62, what **tone** does the writer use in describing the way relatives were informed about their loved ones' death. " (2 marks)

10. In lines 63 – 65 how does **the use of imagery** convey that the author finds the memories of the film are hard to remove? (2 mark)

11. In lines 64 – 69, how does the writer's **use of language** convey the behaviour of both the Americans and the Germans on the beach?

    You should use at least two examples in your answer. (4 marks)

12. Looking at lines 70 –73, how does the writer create an effective ending to the passage? You should look at **word choice** and **ideas** in your answer. (2 marks)

30 Marks

Marks Scheme – War Comes to the Cinema

1.

(a). *Pupils must use their own words as far as possible. Complete quotations = zero marks. One mark for any of the following:*

- The author thought that war films had a moral compass
- The characters who were virtuous won while the ones who were evil lost
- When a main character was killed he delivered a speech to the audience
- Movies were about fairness

(b). *One mark for quotation of word and one mark for appropriate explanation.*

- "deserved" – suggests that, in the author's mind, soldiers died because they were on the wrong side
- "touching" – suggests that when death occurs on the battlefield it is scripted and emotional
- "justice" – suggests that there is a sense of right and wrong in warfare

2. *One mark for a quotation of sentence structure and one mark for explanation.*

- Use of parenthesis "everything was in code to create secrecy" – helps to add extra information and emphasize that the mission was clandestine
- Use of quotation marks "H-hour" – helps to show that the mission used code words in order to keep the details of the landing safe from the Germans

3. *One mark for quotation of word and one mark for appropriate explanation.*

- "bogged down" – suggests the soldiers were open to enemy fire
- "trapped" – suggests the soldiers could not escape the beach
- "struggling" – suggests the solders could not fight back effectively
- "survive" – suggests that many soldiers died during the landings
- "easy target" –suggests the soldiers were enclosed and surrounded on all sides
- "vulnerable – suggests the soldiers were unable to move and exposed on the beach

4. *One mark for quotation / identification of image and one mark for explanation.*

- "Like alert blood hounds" – image helps to reinforce the idea that the Germans were dangerous and ready for the attack

5. *One mark for a quotation / identification of sentence structure and one mark for explanation.*

- Use of parenthesis "no doubt with their morale in mind" – helps to show that general Bradley was concerned for the troops and wanted them to succeed

- Sentence builds to a climax "would weaken and discourage the German defenders" – helps to emphasize that general Bradley thought that the Germans would offer less resistance than what was found

6. *One mark for a quotation / identification of image and one mark for explanation.*

    - "like water from a fire fighter's hose" – helps to emphasize the number of bullets and the force at which they were being fired at the troops on the beaches
    - "It was the Rolls Royce of machine guns" – Rolls Royce is associated with quality engineering, which suggests the guns were well made and capable of destruction

7. *Pupils must use their own words as far as possible. Complete quotations = zero marks. One mark for any of the following:*

    - The special effects are so good that the actions appears real
    - The film is graphic and openly shows the realities of war
    - Soldier seems to die in a believable way

8. *Pupils need only identify how the sentence links forward OR backward for full marks. One mark for quotation and one mark for appropriate explanation.*

    - "Perhaps too graphic for the film" – links back to the ideas in the previous paragraph which discusses "Saving Private Ryan" and its impact on the author
    - "plight of immobile injured soldiers" or "drowned as the tide came in" – links forward to the ideas in the passage which explain the loss of life suffered by the Allies and how families were notified of deaths

9. *One mark for identification of tone. One mark for how the tone is created.*

    - The author's tone is critical / disparaging / negative

    - The use of the unspecified name "Mr and Mrs Smith" or "Mr and Mrs Jones" – helps to highlight that soldiers' lives were not valued; they were expendable
    - Word choice of "awful" – shows the trauma the death of a soldier would have had on the family
    - The explanation that the notice was send out "conventionally in the mail" – emphasizes the number of troops whose families must have been notified of their death and the lack of compassion or sympathy

10. *One mark for a quotation / identification of image and one mark for explanation.*

    - "clings to my memory like a tattoo" – helps to highlight the lasting impression the film had on the writer and conveys a sense of permanence

11. *One mark for quotation / identification of techniques and one more for explanation.*

Word choice

- "cruelly" – suggests that the German's killed with impudence
- "no mercy" – suggests that Germans wanted no one to escape or reach the beach
- "hardened" – suggests that the Americans have few feelings or emotions about killing the enemy troops
- "needlessly" – suggests the Americans killed without need or consideration
- "brutally" – suggests that the Americans inflicted pain and discomfort without need

Sentence Structure

- Use of short sentence "However, neither side plays fair" – highlights that both the German and the Americans inflicted huge casualties on each side and showed a great deal of ruthlessness

12. *Question should be marked on merit. One mark for a basic comment on ideas or techniques and two marks for a more in-depth analysis.*

Possible comments may include:

- The contrast of the weather and the writer's reflection of the film helps to reinforce the film's impact
- The mention of the weather links back to the opening of the passage and the writer going to see the film
- Use of the word "struggles" - again helps to highlight how many men lost their lives on the beaches of Normandy
- Direct last sentence "Once you see it, you cannot forget it" – shows how thought provoking the film is and its legacy

Living off the "fatta the lan'"

In this passage, the writer explores his dreams of owning his own farm and his fond memories of the novel "Of Mice and Men". He also discusses the realities of farming and the hard work that it entails.

Nowadays, we are used to buying all manner of fruit and vegetables in the supermarkets. While once exotic, dragon fruit and mangos are now everywhere. As for something as mundane as a bag of carrots, we expect it to cost little more than a few coins in our pocket. In short, food is easy to come by. Therefore, it's odd that growing your own fruit and vegetables is becoming increasingly popular. As British cities become more urban, more covered in concrete and grey, there seems to be a desire to get back to something basic and understandable, like the simple process of growing food. I love growing my own fruit and vegetables. Planting a few seeds in a raised bed of sweet smelling compost, watching those seeds grow into plants and flowers, and, finally, eating a crop fresh from the ground or picking it right from the stem, is a truly satisfying experience. Whenever I pick fresh peas or lift a crop of new potatoes, I feel like I am connecting with a deep and primitive part of myself.

There are days when, wandering around my small city garden, I imagine myself as a farmer. In my mind, I own a smallholding with old, stone walls and a red tiled roof. Around my perfect little farm the countryside rolls away in shades of amber and green. Near the house there's a walled vegetable garden with rich, weed-free soil. Obviously, in this perfect dream it is always summer – the days are long and lush and last forever. Just thinking of it now makes me let out a wistful sigh.

But I know that there's one glaring problem with this mental picture: I know that owning a farm is a hard life, filled with a tremendous amount of work.

While it might seem odd, I blame John Steinbeck for my pastoral dreams. This is because there's a good chance that the seeds of this idyllic rural life were sown in my mind by the novel "Of Mice and Men". Most of us have read about the two ranch hands, George Milton and Lennie Small, in secondary school. Steinbeck's novel captivated me then and still captivates me now. In the book the two men want nothing more than to own their own farm and to "live off the fatta the lan'". Long before the grow-your-own movement took hold, George and Lennie were wandering around the fields of California looking for a place to call their own. For a long time, I've been wandering with them.

Before anyone jumps to the obvious joke, yes I am probably more like Lennie then George. However, I am smart enough at least to know this: farming is difficult work. Farmers work long hours in all types of weather to bring food to our tables. In short, while I enjoy growing some fruit and vegetables for the table, some part of me knows that, I would make a terrible farmer. Therefore I do what most gardeners do – I have a vegetable patch were I can grow a few things while safely relying on those who actually know what they're doing; the farmers.

35 This spring however, my inner Lennie got the better of me. I bought chickens. My purchase wasn't just on a whim. I had a space at the end of my garden. I researched the cost and equipment necessary to keep three chickens. I learned about their needs and requirements and how to keep them healthy. Still, I felt apprehensive when we drove up to a local farm and arrived back home with our three new hens. I wondered if I'd made the right decision?

40 The first night I introduced the hens to their new home I was nervous. We have foxes in our neighbourhood, and I was worried that they'd swarm on the coop in some kind of feeding frenzy the moment they smelt the birds. That first night I tiptoed, slippers wet from the lawn, several times back and forth to the henhouse to make sure the "girls" were okay. The next morning, when all three chickens emerged from their house alive, I was relived. To top it all
45 off, later that morning we had our first egg. My daughter was ecstatic. We took a picture (yes, of an egg).

So would I ever move to the countryside? Could I ever really make it as a farmer? The answer is, obviously, no. I don't have any plans yet to "live off the fatta the lan'". However, with the world moving faster and faster, and as technological advancements erupt around us
50 like unpredictable volcanos, there is a part of me which longs for the good life. I don't think I'm the only one who, faced with 24 hour news and the constant threat of terrorist attacks, desires something simpler and more easily understood. Growing fruit and vegetables, and keeping a few chickens, is a life-affirming act which benefits both the environment and the people living in it. Maybe one day, I'll even buy a few rabbits – there's a space near the back
55 of the garden for a small hutch.

Tom Smart – originally published in The Guardian

Questions – Living off the "fatta the lan'"

1. Read lines 1 – 11

   a. **In your own words**, how to people currently feel about buying food at a supermarket? (2 marks)

   b. **Explain** why there is a desire for people to grow their own food? (2 marks)

2. How does the **word choice** of lines 7 – 12 create a positive impression of growing food? (2 marks)
3. 3. How do lines 19 – 20 act as a **link** in the passage? (2 marks)
4. 4. **Summarise** the reasons in lines 21 – 28 for why the author has a desire to grow his own food. (3 marks)
5. How does the **language** in lines 29 – 34 help to make clear that the author knows that farm life can be challenging? (4 marks)
6. Read lines 33 – 34. **In your own words**, how does the author balance his desire to grow food with his want of a comfortable life? (2 marks)
7. In lines 35 – 39, the author gets ready for the arrival of his new chickens. **Summarise** the steps he takes before he purchases the hens. (3 marks)
8. What is the author's **tone** in lines 43 – 47? How is the tone created? (2 marks)
9. How does the **sentence structure** of lines 47 – 48 help to make clear that the author does not think he would make a good farmer? (2 marks)
10. How does the **imagery** of lines 49 – 53 help make clear that the author feels that the pace of change in our modern lives can be frightening? (2 marks)
11. How does the author's use of **word choice** in lines 53 – 55 help to emphasize his positive view of gardening and growing food. (2 marks)
12. How **effective** do you find the final paragraph as a conclusion to the article? (2 marks)

30 Marks

Marks Scheme - Living off the "fatta the lan'"

1.

a. *Pupils must use their own words as far as possible. Complete quotations = zero marks. One mark for any of the following:*

- People find that there is a wide selection
- Food once seen as strange or foreign is now common
- Buying fruit or vegetables is seen as inexpensive

b. *Pupils must use their own words as far as possible. Complete quotations = zero marks. One mark for any of the following:*

- Cities are become more densely populated and less green
- Growing your own food is not difficult or complex to comprehend
- Growing fruit and vegetables is relatively easy process
- Seeing plants grow and harvesting food is rewarding

2. *One mark for a quotation / identification of word and one mark for explanation.*

- "desire" – suggests that growing vegetables is something people are naturally inclined to do
- "understandable" – suggests that growing food can be achieved without the need of complex instruction or extensive education
- "sweet smelling" – suggests that vegetable and fruit growing is a pleasant experience
- "satisfying" – suggests that the act of growing food brings joy and happiness

3. *Pupils must identify how the sentence either links forward or backward. One mark for quotation and one mark for explanation.*

- "one glaring problem with the mental picture" – links back to the author's desire to live on a farm and the image he holds in his mind
- "hard life, filled with a tremendous amount of work" – links forward to the author's discussion about how he came to want a farm and his appreciation that being a farmer is a difficult life

4. *Pupils must use their own words as far as possible. Complete quotations = zero marks. One mark for any of the following:*

- The author read the book "Of Mice and Men" when he was younger
- He loved the book and found it fascinating
- In the novel, the two main characters also dream of owning a farm and being self-sufficient

5. *One mark for identification of technique and one mark for explanation.*

Word Choice

- "difficult" – suggests that the work done of farms is strenuous and physically demanding
- "long hours" – suggests that farming is a lifestyle which takes dedication and lots of manual labour

Sentence structure

- Use of colon "…at least to know this: farming is difficult work." – The use of a colon helps to create a pause which emphasizes the author's view that working the land is challenging and at times unforgiving
- Use of semi-colon "…they're doing; the farmers." – juxtaposition of the two thoughts helps to highlight the author's view that he lacks the appropriate knowledge to be a farmer

6. *Pupils must use their own words as far as possible. Complete quotations = zero marks.*

- The author grows some edible crops
- Does not rely on his own abilities to grow food for survival – he leaves that to proper farmers

7. *Pupils must use their own words as far as possible. Complete quotations = zero marks. One mark for any of the following:*

- He made sure he had the appropriate space
- The author looked into the amount of money it would take in order to feed and keep chickens
- The author sourced the necessary supplies, housing and food
- He found out how to care for chickens and their living requirements

8. *One mark for identification of tone and one mark for identification of techniques with appropriate explanation.*

The tone is humorous.

The author creates this by using:

- Parenthesis "slippers wet from the lawn" – a comical image of being outdoors in a dressing gown
- Use of quotation marks around "girls" – helps to make the chickens seem more human / part of the family
- Use of parenthesis "(yes, of an egg)" – highlights the excitement of the finding an egg, even though it is an ordinary foodstuff

9. *One mark for identification of sentence structure and one mark for explanation.*

- Use of rhetorical questions "So would I never move the countryside?" – helps to underline the fact that he author does not think he would truly suit rural life
- Short sentence "The answer is, obviously, no." – answers the author's own question and emphasizes his realisation that he is not a farmer

10. *One mark for identification of image and one mark for explanation.*

- "erupting around us like unpredictable volcanos" – a volcano is a dangerous and violent natural event. This therefore highlights the dangerous an volatile nature of technology

11. *One mark for identification of technique and one mark for explanation.*

Word choice

- "life-affirming" – suggests that growing food helps both the mind and body
- "benefits" – suggests that vegetable and fruit growing is productive and helps the natural world

12. *Pupils may refer to content or technique in order to support their viewpoint.*

Possible comments may include:

- The use of a series of rhetorical questions helps to engage the reader and make them consider their own view of rural life
- The quote from the novel "Of Mice and Men" links back to the author's like of John Steinbeck
- The use of imagery – "violent volcanos" – creates and effective contrast between the pace of modern life and the simplicity of gardening
- The mention of rabbits connects to the novel "Of Mice and Men"

Scots Language Surrender

In this passage the author ponders the differences in accents that exist across the United Kingdom, and the discrimination with which accents can be viewed.

The uneasy union of nations that is Scotland and England is further strained by the issue of accents and speaking properly. The gulf between a southern received pronunciation and the traditional Scots accent is wide and made wider by a broadcasting standard established before World War II. Like a linguistic form of the old school tie*, broadcasters placed emphasis on
5 the way you said things, not what you said. This tendency created a battleground on which the traditional Scots language was bound to be the loser.

The ability to speak with a clipped, precise English accent was a clear indication that you had a good education; and if you wanted to read the news, or indeed broadcast anything verbally, it was a necessity. If you - born in Glasgow, Dundee or Inverness - did not have the correct
10 sounds coming from between your lips then there wasn't much point knocking on the door of Broadcasting House*, looking for a job.

There is no need to investigate this. We do not need any leaked policy documents for confirmation of BBC standards on this matter. We get a sharper reminder of old broadcasting voices every time we see any black and white footage of post-war Scottish cup Finals. Had
15 they been commentating then, Richard Gordon or Pat Nevin would not have given any coverage, despite their knowledge of the game. Back then the commentary was handled by a chap speaking perfect BBC English. If he was remotely Scottish, he did a great job of covering it up. Richard and Pat would not have had the correct vocal sounds, too many rolling "rs"; just too Scottish-sounding for the job. They could have done the lighting, the
20 camera work, but not anything near the microphone. Sorry lads, you would not have sounded right!

Things have changed since then and all kinds of regional accents are on the screen and the radio, but we Scots might have had a claim of discrimination upheld in court had it all turned out differently. Maybe we still have a case? It is almost impossible for many of us north of
25 the border to achieve that old BBC accent unless we are actors with a skill for mimicking accents.

Today the Scots do get behind the microphone on merit, but some damage has been done with all of this. A pecking order of accents has emerged. I remember an interview with Sting many years ago. Sting was the singer in the 1980s group "The Police". Someone asked him
30 why he no longer spoke with a northern accent. He is originally from Newcastle. Sting explained that when he moved to London people were having difficulty understanding him, so he decided to change his accent completely.

Sting's radical change of voice highlights the pressure on northerners to make their language "better" and "clearer", rather than a problem with accents. A different accent is only rarely
35 the reason why we don't understand people. Certain words and phrases can seem strange to those not brought up with them but the notion that dialects and regional accents make English

impossible to understand is a myth. A northerner's feeling of inferiority is understandable nevertheless when only "posh" accents read the news or do "intelligent" documentaries.

While one famous singer may have felt it necessary to change his way of speaking, what has
40 happened in Scotland is in some ways more alarming. Our linguistic surrender has been almost unconditional. We accept the quality of Robert Burns' poetry, for example, yet downgrade the Scots language he wrote with as colloquial or "slang". In schools you are taught to write essays formally; in reality these essays would seem strange, especially in exams, were they to contain traditional Scots. It was all right for Robert Burns, but is not
45 good enough English to put in your jotter.

Words like "drookit" or "dreich" may appear in the playground where we listen with or "lugs" or talk of "tatties" and "neeps" but increasingly, if we even know them, we regard these words and others as quaint and informal – not to be used in formal situations. The language of the south has been dominant for decades. No broadcaster has become a news
50 anchor in the UK with a Scottish or for that matter Northern Irish accent. Celtic sounds are, it seems, for the regions. The fact that we don't publicly admit that doesn't mean that it is not true. We then deal it all a final blow by trying to talk "properly" ourselves. The result is not complicated: back in the playground today's Scottish children would struggle to tell you five or six traditional Scottish words for things.

55 We see examples of our own lack of confidence regularly. A witness, interviewed in front of camera at the scene of an accident will "up" their language immediately: "outside the hoose" becomes "outside the house"; the "wee lassie" who was the subject of the accident, will become "a little girl"; this immediate alteration because a microphone is pointed at our mouths. To stick to what was once our normal idiom for the telly, or in an interview situation
60 where a job is at stake, would be dangerous. It might not sound right, we feel.

In an ideal world we should be able to speak naturally, not self-consciously, but reality is rarely ideal. It should be our own language we defend and express: "hooses", "lassies" and all the rest of it. It is a language with its own characteristics, words and sounds. When a southerner comes north we do not expect them to change to Scots. Why should we have felt
65 for years that we need to alter our own language? English would be dealt a severe blow without Latin at its roots and French dangling from its branches.

So what has happened to Scots? Where is our northern tongue, in place for centuries, in the scheme of things? In many places you will not hear it at all. French words and phrases were considered more acceptable, routinely added to English, while Latin was seen as more
70 valuable: Scots was a non-starter. Is that what happened? Whatever the answer, Scots is your downgraded tongue, set aside as no more than a local idiom. It is ideal for those who are familiar with it, but not elsewhere.

Things will of course change in Scotland in the future but our language as it once was has surrendered. Only little traces are scattered about. In major cities, among the trendy, the
75 undergraduates, in the language of business or law, Scots has gone. Even our distinctive accent has been sandpapered down to a Scottish/English when we want to talk "properly", that is. It was once at the root of what many of us know of language but it is hard to see,

beyond the limits of a school project or an academic study, how it can be brought back to proud and general use.

*old school tie – was a system where posh schools were favoured and helped to get a good job. Often a school tie was worn at a job interview in order to influence the people interviewing you.

*Broadcasting House – was the headquarters of the BBC.

James Getty – originally published in The Press and Journal

Questions – Scots Language Surrender

1. In lines 4 – 6, what does the writer mean when he says: *"…broadcasters placed emphasis on the way you said things, not what you said"?* **Use your own words** in your answer. (2 marks)
2. *"This tendency created a battleground…"* lines 6 – 7; what does the writer's **imagery** suggest about the way the Scot's language has been disregarded? (3 marks)
3. In lines 7 – 11, and, **using your own words**, explain why there was not *"…any point"* in *"knocking"* on the *"door of Broadcasting House."* (2 marks)
4. In lines 12 – 21, why does the writer not need to investigate the issue of the Scots language not being suitable? (2 marks)
5. Look at lines 18 – 21. In your **own words** explain what would have been wrong with Richard Gordon's or Pat Nevin's accent. (2 marks)
6. In lines 27 – 28, according to the writer, what has changed in broadcasting? **Use your own words.** (2 marks)
7. What is it *"almost impossible"*, lines 24 – 26, for Scottish people to do? **Use your own words.** (1 mark)
8. How does the first sentence in paragraph five, lines 27 – 28, *"Today the Scots do…damage been done."* act as a **link**? (2 marks)
9. How does the writer's **word choice**, lines 33 – 38 show that he does not think regional accents are a problem? (2 marks)
10. In lines 64 – 65, how does the writer's **sentence structure** help to convey his attitude to changing your accent? (2 marks)
11. Look at lines 65 – 66, *"English would be dealt…dangling from its branches"* How does the writer's **imagery** convey the different elements contained in a language. (2 marks)
12. Look at lines 70 – 72 and, **using your own words**, explain what has happened to Scots. (2 marks)
13. Look at lines 73 – 77, how does **word choice** convey the writer's feelings about the fate of Scots? (4 marks)
14. Look at the end of the passage, lines 73 – 79. How does this create an effective ending to the writer's argument? (2 marks)

30 marks

Answers – Scots Language Surrender

1. *Pupils must use their own words as far as possible. Complete quotations = zero marks. One mark for any of the following:*

    - The way you sounded mattered
    - You had to have a posh accent
    - What you expressed was not as important as the way you sounded

2. *One mark for a quotation / identification of image and one mark for explanation.*

    - "created a battleground" – suggests that there were victims and losers, just like in warfare. This helps to emphasize that broadcasters could be both ruthless and unpleasant.

3. *Pupils must use their own words as far as possible. Complete quotations = zero marks. One mark for any of the following:*

    - The headquarters were not interested in regional accents
    - People with regional accents did not go on the airwaves
    - The headquarters were judgemental of people with accents which did not sound posh

4. *Pupils must use their own words as far as possible. Complete quotations = zero marks. One mark for any of the following:*

    - Every time he watches coverage of an old football match, the commentator is very posh
    - The commentators are typically not Scottish
    - Most commentators did not have a regional accent

5. *Pupils must use their own words as far as possible. Complete quotations = zero marks. One mark for any of the following:*

    - They do not sound posh enough
    - Their accents are too strong
    - They did not have the correct voice to broadcast

6. *Pupils must use their own words as far as possible. Complete quotations = zero marks. One mark for any of the following:*

- A variety /several types of voices are used these days
- There is more of an acceptance of regional accents

7. *Pupils must use their own words as far as possible. Complete quotations = zero marks. One mark for any of the following:*

   - Cannot sound different
   - Unable to change their voice or change their way of speaking

8. *Pupils must identify how the sentence either links forward or backward. One mark for quotation and one mark for explanation.*

   - "Today the Scots do get behind the microphone…" – links back to the idea that Scots once did not get near a microphone
   - "some damage has been done with all this" – links forward to the idea of Sting/northerners feeling they should change their accent as it has limited value

9. *One mark for identification of a word and one mark for explanation.*

   - "rarely the reason" – suggests they seldom cause problems
   - "the notion that…regional accents make English hard to understand is a myth" – suggests it is not true that a variety of accents cause communication problems
   - "notion" – suggests a half-formed thought
   - "myth" – suggests an idea that is not in fact true

10. *One mark for a quotation of sentence structure and one mark for explanation.*

    - Use of rhetorical question "Why should we have felt for years that we need to alter our language?" – asks the reader to think about how ridiculous/unreasonable/bizarre/strange/unnatural it is to change your accent because those around you do not share it

11. *One mark for a quotation / identification of image and one mark for explanation.*

    - "Latin at its roots" – helps to reinforce the fact that Latin is the base / core of the English language; a trees grows from its roots as English grew from Latin

12. *Pupils must use their own words as far as possible. Complete quotations = zero marks. One mark for any of the following:*

- It has been scaled down put to one side as no more than a local way of speaking
- It is good for people who know it or use it, but nowhere else

13. *One mark for identification of a word and one mark for explanation.*

- "surrendered" – suggests it is defeated/given up
- "only little traces" – suggests only small parts remain
- "scattered about" – suggests it is all broken up/chaotic/disorganised
- "gone" – suggests definite/emphatic word choice suggesting this is a fact

14. *Question should be marked on merit. One mark for a basic comment on ideas or techniques and two marks for a more in-depth analysis.*

Possible comments may include:

- Returns to idea of the core or *"root"* of what was once the language
- Imagery of *"sandpapered down"* suggests it has been wiped out/eroded/rubbed away etc.
- Returns to the idea expressed earlier comparing language to a tree
- Suggests that it is impossible for the language to be brought back to use generally, suggesting *"surrender"*, just as the title suggested

An American in Scotland

In this passage the author writes about moving to Scotland from America. He highlights the differences between the two countries, and how the election of Donald Trump in the United States has confused and upset him.

I'm an American. I now live in the United Kingdom. Eleven years ago, I left the baking red heat of the Arizona desert for the soggy green hills of Scotland. The reason for my emigration was an excuse as old as humanity: love. I'd met a girl from Scotland. We got married in a cross-Atlantic swirl of confused accents and too much whisky. We bought a house. I got a job.
5 We now have two young children.

I like living in the UK. I like the people and I like the place. Yes, February is bleak and my tan has long since faded, but Great Britain has offered me opportunities which I would have never had in the United States. I can see a doctor – for free. I was able to attend a good university for a very reasonable price – free. When I went to get a prescription for an infection the
10 pharmacist told me the cost, "Free". I still remember when my first employer told me my holiday entitlement was 30 days. I was baffled. I wondered, do these people realise they're giving me over a month off, paid? Beyond the constant drizzle, I began to understand that there was a real difference between America and Scotland.

However, even with all these positive aspects of my new life, it has always been hard to shake
15 the feeling that behind me, I've left a better life. Indeed, when I tell people I'm from the west coast of American they look at me quizzically. Then comes the inevitable question, "Why are you living here?" The suggestion is always the same: isn't America – even with all of its flaws – better? It's a question I do ask myself. Growing up in America, we were raised on dreams and the idea that you could become whatever you wanted. It's an idea which goes back to the
20 roots of the country. There's ways been the notion of the American Dream; the land of milk and honey. America has always been seen as a place where anyone can become a Jay Gatsby; work hard enough and you too will be a success. In short, a better tomorrow was always just over the next horizon.

On a cold Scottish evening, sitting next to a trembling radiator, it's hard to escape the ideas on
25 which I was raised. Maybe I just watched too much television as a kid, but there are days I really miss America. Occasionally, I've brought up the question with my wife about moving back "home". We've talked about it in the past, but she doesn't want to leave her family behind, and now that the kids are settled in school, I'm definitely here to stay. But every time my social media buzzes with a picture of a Californian beach or a New York skyline, a little
30 butterfly in my stomach waves its wings.

Then came the election of Donald Trump. My colleagues at work laughed about his running; I dismissed it. He then became the official nominee for the Republican Party; I criticized it. In the early hours in the morning after the vote, when it became clear Trump had won, I denied

it. I think a part of me is in denial still. What I have seen recently has made me feel further
35 from home then I have felt in the last eleven years.

Donald Trump is the polar opposite of everything I've told myself I miss about America. That optimistic, kind, free-spirited America I left behind has been replaced with chaos, bigotry, and suspicion. The American I left, the one I knew, didn't openly support the torture of prisoners. Shockingly, it happened, but everyone I spoke to was horrified by the revelations that the
40 government committed acts of torture and waterboarding. Trump now openly agrees with it.

The America I left behind did feel xenophobic and isolationist. Admittedly, racism is a part of American history and still very much exists. However, I never thought the American people would vote to literally wall themselves in. The America I thought I knew wasn't misogynistic and mean. Yes, equality was a long way off but I never believed a politician could openly brag
45 about abusing women and still win power. In short, America has always had its flaws, but the radical now seems to have become mainstream – it's as if those on the fringe have somehow gotten hold of the microphone.

I've not been back to the United States for four years. Between the cost of flights and the kids, it's been too difficult to make the journey. The election of Trump has made me wonder, if I do
50 ever go back to the US, will it be anything like the country I remember? It's very easy to view the past through rose-tinted spectacles, and perhaps, over the years, I've created a sanitised view of the America I want to remember. But I do remember it as a happy place, as a place which was, for lack of a better word, good. It seems like, somewhere between the mass shootings, violent police officers, and a megalomaniac in the White House, everything has
55 changed. I wonder where all the kindness went? While I'm sure that the earth is the same size it was eleven years, ago, it just feels like home is much further away.

Tom Smart – original published in The Scotsman

<u>**Questions – An American in Scotland**</u>

1. How does the author's use of **sentence structure** in lines 1 – 5 help to emphasize the reason he left America for Scotland? (2 marks)
2. How does the author's use of **contrast** in lines 1 – 2 help to highlight the dramatic change in his life when he moved to Scotland? (2 marks)
3. How does the author's **use of language** in lines 6 – 12 help to reinforce the reasons he enjoys living in the United Kingdom? (4 marks)
4. In lines 15 – 19, what is people's reaction when they find out he is an American living in Britain? Use your **own words** as far as possible. (2 marks)
5. Look at lines 19 – 24. Summarise the key belief or idea that the author feels he grew up with. What does he feel many Americans believe about their country? (2 marks)
6. According to lines 25 – 29, why does the author believe that he will never move back to the United States? Use your **own words** as far as possible. (2 marks)
7. How does the author's use of **imagery** in lines 29 - 31 help to reinforce the fact that the author still misses America? (2 marks)
8. How does the **sentence structure** in lines 32 – 36 help to emphasize the author's shock at Donald Trump becoming the president of the United States? (2 marks)
9. Read lines 37 – 48. In your **own words**, how does the author believe his home country has changed? (4 marks)
10. What is the author's tone in lines 42 – 48? How is the tone created? (2 marks)
11. In your **own words**, summarise the reasons the author gives in lines 49 – 50 for not returned to America for four years? (2 marks)
12. How does the author's **use of language** in lines 50 – 57 help emphasize his fear that America has changed beyond recognition? (4 marks)

30 Marks

Answers – An American in Scotland

1. *One mark for identification of sentence structure and one mark for explanation.*

   - Use of colon "…excuse as old as humanity: love." – The colon helps to create a pause and emphasize the information which follows. The punctuation helps to reinforce the fact that the author moved to Scotland because he fell in love with a woman
   - Short sentence "I'd met a girl form Scotland." – The short sentence is a simple yet effective statement which highlights that the author left the United States in order to get married

2. *One mark for identification of either side of the contrast. One mark for an appropriate explanation.*

   - "baking red heat of the Arizona desert" contrasts with "soggy green hills of Scotland" – helps to show the difference in the climate of the two countries and implies that there is a big difference between both countries

3. *One mark for identification of language technique and one mark for an appropriate explanation.*

   Word Choice

   - "Opportunities" – helps to suggest that the author feels that living in the UK allows him a better quality of life and greater life chances
   - "Free" – helps to highlight that many of the services available in Scotland are expensive in America

   Sentence Structure

   - Use of the short sentence "I like living in the UK" – The short sentence helps to convey in a simple yet effective statement that the author believes that his quality of life is better in Scotland
   - Use of the dash "I can see a doctor – for free". The dash creates a pause and highlights what comes after; helps to show how impressed the author is that many social services are free
   - Repetition of the word "free" – This helps to underline many of the benefits which Britain offers, cost money in the United States
   - Use of rhetorical question "….giving me a month off, paid?" – The rhetorical question helps to emphasize how amazed the author was by the generous holiday offered to UK employees

4. *Pupils must use their own words as far as possible. Complete quotations = zero marks. One mark for any of the following:*

    - People are shocked / surprised by his decision to live in the UK
    - Many people assume that life is better in the US and wonder about his motives for moving

5. *Pupils must use their own words as far as possible. Complete quotations = zero marks. One mark for any of the following:*

    - The author grew up with the idea that he could achieve anything
    - Hard work will lead to success
    - America is a successful country and full of opportunity
    - Progress and prosperity are possible / common

6. *Pupils must use their own words as far as possible. Complete quotations = zero marks. One mark for any of the following:*

    - The writer's wife does not want to move away from her family – the distance is too great
    - The author's children are attending local school and he does not want to disrupt their education

7. *One mark for quotation / identification of image and one mark for explanation.*

    - Metaphor "a little butterfly in my stomach waves its wings" – the image helps to underline the fact that the author has a deep emotional connection to his home country and this triggers a very real physical response

8. *One mark for quotation / identification of sentence structure and one mark for explanation.*

    - The author's use of semi-colon "…nominee for the Republican Party; I criticized it." – The use of a dash creates a pause emphasising the information which comes after and highlights the writer's anger at the political situation in the US
    - Repetition of the word "denial" – this helps to highlight that the author cannot understand why people voted for Donal Trump and his shock at his election

9. *Pupils must use their own words as far as possible. Complete quotations = zero marks. One mark for any of the following:*

    - The author feels that America has become less tolerant

- He thinks that America is not as welcoming and friendly
- The writer feels that the United States has become more violent and is even willing to commit war crimes
- He believes that the US is not as open to immigrants or foreigners
- He feels that America has become more sexist and less equal for women
- He thinks that America has become more conservative and right-wing

10. *One mark for identification of tone. One mark for an explanation of how the tone is created.*

- The author's tone is critical
- The author's use of critical word choice "xenophobic" and "isolationist" – helps to highlight his feelings of dismay and anger at the changes taking place in America
- The author's use of a dash "....radical now seems to have become mainstream – it's as if those..." helps to emphasize his final dramatic statement / underline the fact that the wrong people are in charge
- The use of imagery "have somehow gotten hold of the microphone" – this helps to underline that the author believes that radical groups now control the government

11. *Pupils must use their own words as far as possible. Complete quotations = zero marks. One mark for any of the following:*

- The flights to the United States are too expensive
- His children are too young / it would be difficult to travel such a long distance with them

12. *One mark for identification of language technique and one mark for an appropriate explanation.*

Sentence structure

- Use of rhetorical question "...will it be anything like the country I remember?" – helps to emphasize that the author is afraid that his country has changed too much or too rapidly
- Rhetorical questions "I wonder where all the kindness went?" – shows the author's fear that America has changed into a cruel and intolerant place
- Use of a list "...between the mass shootings, violent police officers, and a megalomaniac in the White House..." – emphasizes the number of things the author feels is wrong with America and the extent his country has changed

Word Choice

- "sanitised view" – makes clear that the author doubts whether the America he remembers is just in his imagination
- "happy place" – emphasizes the author has fond memories of the US and fears it is changing for the worse
- "violent" – helps to reinforce the idea that the author feels America is becoming a more dangerous place

Imagery

- Metaphor "rose-tinted spectacles" – helps to underline the author's fear that the country he remembers was only a figment of his imagination

Minding the Great Outdoors

In this article the author talks about the benefits of mindfulness and his love of the outdoors. Mindfulness is a form of meditation which encourages the practitioner to be fully aware of the present moment.

Many of us have had a perfect day in the countryside, the kind of day that we hope would never end. A day when the flowers burn brightly with colour, and the trees and shrubs stand green against the blue sky. A day when the grass is soft and rolling. A day when there is a warm sweetness in the air while you wander through the Great British outdoors. It's a kind of day that leaves you feeling calm, collected, and content.

If you've ever had a day like this, there's a good chance you've achieved, at least for a few moments, a mental state known as mindfulness. In the last few years, mindfulness has had a great deal of media attention. Simply put, mindfulness is about being more aware of what is happening both inside and outside ourselves. Mindfulness stems from eastern Buddhist traditions and practices. In the west, it has been embraced and modified and is now considered a useful tool to help focus the mind. Many have found it particularly useful for mental health problems, and it is recommended for issues from anxiety to depression. Even the NHS has endorsed mindfulness. Their website states that, "Becoming more aware of the present moment can help us enjoy the world around us more and understand ourselves better." There are now hundreds of books on how to become more mindful. There are classes being offered in church halls and offices. There are apps, CDs, DVDs and YouTube videos.

For me, the perfect activity to truly become mindful, the thing which allows me to genuinely engage with the world around me, is something I can find right outside the back door – nature. I do practise mindfulness meditation in the classic way (eyes closed and belly breathing), and I have found it to be very useful. I've even been known to light the clichéd stick of incense or two. In short, guided meditation is good. But nothing connects me more to my surroundings than taking a stroll in a local park or walking through the countryside. People have long turned to nature for a bit of peace and relaxation. I know that on a good day, when the sun is shining and fresh air is filling my lungs, I feel totally connected to the present moment. There is a calm in being outdoors, in a green space, which cannot be found anywhere else.

My peace comes in a long walk through the countryside. With my boots laced up and a bottle of water in my rucksack, I love a summer walk through the green hills of Scotland. Whether it's on a sandy beach or along the banks of a babbling burn; being near nature is medicine for the mind. When I'm outdoors, my thoughts seem to become smooth and level like the open sea. At this point I have entered what psychologists call "flow": a term used to describe a person's state of mind when they are completely absorbed in an activity. The feeling of flow is closely associated with mindfulness. When I'm lost in nature few things can draw my attention.

35 Trite as it may sound, I feel as if all the individual threads of my mind are woven properly together by interacting with nature. We're taught in school that humans have five major senses (though in reality I'm told there are many more), and if mindfulness means being fully aware of the world around you, fully engaged with your senses, then I can think of no better environment than a forest or an open field to become more mindful in. Being outside gives us 40 a chance to disconnect from the chaotic modern world, to close our eyes, bend down, and inhale the gentle fragrance of a flower. I remember one summer walking though the Highlands and stumbling across a tangle of ripe, wild raspberries. I ate so many that my hands were sticky and red from their juices; my lips were coated with the lipstick of nature. Then there's the other senses: the dazzling sight of cherry blossom in spring or the sound of 45 grasses dancing in an autumn breeze.

These experiences are not the preserve of the elite; nature is all around us. I live in a quiet suburb attached to a larger city. I don't have a great rural estate or private lands. There is nothing exclusive or expensive about going for a walk. And that, is the beauty of it; going for a stroll, for example, is an activity which is available to almost anyone. Interacting with 50 nature could even be something as simple as stepping out the back door. Most of us do not have acres of land, but around 90% of British households do have access to some kind of garden or open space. With a little bit of effort we may all be able to find our little piece of Zen.

Nature and mindfulness seem like a perfect match. There are so many aspects of modern life 55 which people seem to disconnect from – long monotone office meetings, spreadsheet filled computer screens, cramped train rides or traffic jams. Due to the stressful and fractured nature of life, people often want to be somewhere else. It doesn't need to be like this. If you want something that reconnects you to the world around you, which makes you more mindful of the present moment, then look no further than the green grass, or the stony path beneath 60 your feet. You really will not find a better meditation mat.

Tom Smart –originally published in The Guardian

Questions - Minding the Great Outdoors

1. In lines 1 – 5, how does the **author's use of language** help to create a pleasant picture of the countryside? (4 marks)
2. Read lines 6 – 11. **Explain both** what mindfulness is and its origins. (2 marks)
3. Looking at lines 15 – 16, how does the author's use of **sentence structure** help to emphasize the popularity of mindfulness? (2 marks)
4. How does the author's **sentence structure** in lines 17 – 19 help to highlight the connection between mindfulness and the natural world? (2 marks)
5. Referring to lines 21 – 26, in your own words, how does the author feel when he engages with nature? (2 marks)
6. How does the **imagery** in lines 30 – 31 help to emphasize how the author feels when he is surrounded by nature? (2 marks)
7. Looking at lines 31 – 34, **in your own words**, explain the mental state known as "flow". (2 mark)
8. How does **the imagery** in lines 35 – 36 help to reinforce the author's feeling about mindfulness and nature? (2 marks)
9. Why, according to the author in lines 36 – 45, does nature help make him more mindful? Answer in **your own words**. (4 marks)
10. Look at lines 46 – 53. **In your own words** explain why the author believes that the benefits of mindfulness and nature are accessible to everyone? (4 marks)
11. Why, according to lines 54 – 56, are nature and mindfulness so relevant to "modern life"? (2 marks)
12. How is the final sentence of the article (line 60) an effective conclusion to the passage as a whole? You should look at **language** and **ideas** in your answer. (2 marks)

30 Marks

Answers – Minding the Great Outdoors

1. *One mark for quotation / identification of techniques and one more for explanation.*

   Word Choice

   - "perfect" – suggests untouched beauty
   - "never end" – suggests that it's an experience / that it is wonderful
   - "soft and rolling" – suggests an attractive natural environment
   - "warm sweetness" – suggests a pleasant countryside scene

   Sentence Structure

   - Repetition of "A day" – helps to reinforce that idea that spending time in the countryside creates memorable experiences
   - List "…feeling calm, collected, and content." – helps to make clear that time spent connecting with nature is beneficial both mentally and physically

   Imagery

   - "flowers burn brightly with colour" – comparing the flowers to a fire, which helps to highlight the brilliance of the natural environment
   - "trees and shrubs stand green against the blue sky" – personification helps to underline the majesty of the scene

2. *Pupils must use their own words as far as possible. Complete quotations = zero marks. One mark for any of the following:*

   - Mindfulness is a person being attentive to their surrounding situation and their internal emotional state
   - Mindfulness originated in "The East" (accept China or Asia or associated countries) – it comes from Buddhist beliefs and practices

3. *One mark for a quotation of sentence structure and one mark for explanation.*

   - Repetition of "There are" – helps to underline the fact that mindfulness is very prevalent in society
   - List "There are apps, CDs, DVDs and YouTube videos." – shows the number of resources that people can now access if they are interested in mindfulness

4. *One mark for a quotation of sentence structure and one mark for explanation.*

- Use of parenthesis "the thing which allows me to genuinely engage with the world around me" – helps to highlight the author's opinion that there is a tangible connection between nature and mindfulness
- Use of the dash "…I can find right outside the back door – nature." – creates a pause which emphasizes the word "nature"; helps to reinforce the link between outside spaces and mindfulness

5. *Pupils must use their own words as far as possible. Complete quotations = zero marks. One mark for any of the following:*

- The author feels aware and able to fully appreciate the present
- The author feels tranquil / peaceful / quiet

6. *One mark for quotation / identification of image and one mark for explanation.*

- "thoughts become smooth and level like the open sea" – the simile helps to emphasize the effect that nature has on the author's emotional and mental state – it makes him more calm and peaceful

7. *Pupils must use their own words as far as possible. Complete quotations = zero marks. One mark for any of the following*:

- A deep thought process or connected state
- A person is totally involved with what they are doing / a task

8. *One mark for quotation / identification of image and one mark for explanation.*

- "…individual threads of my mind are woven properly together…" – metaphor helps to highlight the author's belief that being outdoors helps to focus the mind and improve mental health generally

9. *Pupils must use their own words as far as possible. Complete quotations = zero marks. One mark for any of the following:*

- Being outdoors involves all of the author's five senses, allowing him to be more mindful
- Nature allows the author to remove himself from the stresses of modern life and therefore be more mindful
- The outdoors gives the author a chance to interact with nature - smelling flowers or eating berries, for example, which makes him more mindful
- Interacting with nature allows the author to see the beauty of nature, making him more mindful

10. *Pupils must use their own words as far as possible. Complete quotations = zero marks. One mark for any of the following:*

- The author does not have a large property, nor does he live in the countryside
- It does not cost money to go for a walk or to interact with nature – it is a free activity
- Nature is right outside most people's back door – it is readily available
- Most British homes have gardens or are near green space

11. *Pupils must use their own words as far as possible. Complete quotations = zero marks. One mark for any of the following:*

- Many people do not enjoy a lot of their lives / the way we live now disappoints
- Working on computers (Spreadsheets), boring office work, or riding on trains are all stressful – mindfulness and nature work against these things
- Many people want to be elsewhere and don't enjoy the present

12. *Question should be marked on merit. One mark for a basic comment on ideas or techniques and two marks for a more in-depth analysis.*

- Short sentence "You really will not find a better meditation mat." – clear simple conclusion and summary of the author's ideas / appreciation of nature and mindfulness
- "meditation mat" – imagery which connects the grass and paths in nature to mindfulness; this successfully summarises the author's link between these two things
- "meditation mat" – alliteration creates a memorable phrase
- Ends on a positive or upbeat tone – effectively helps to persuade the reader that they too should engage more with nature

Hunting for Bargains is Complicated

In this article the author considers the nature of consumerism. Reflecting on a time when he thought he purchased a bargain, the author comes to realise that he might have been manipulated.

Usually taking up half the window, the poster with the word "SALE" on it is a magnet for the public. Its force is such that reluctant spenders, those who avoid shops and head in their leisure time for football terraces or a walk in the hills, will come to town just for a bargain, or just curiously to see if it is true that prices really have been "halved" and "slashed" as the
5 adverts always say.

Bargains are made of the stock that would not sell for the original price so selling at a discount is the best way a retailer can get items - usually piled pyramid-high in the stock room - over the counter in exchange for some money in the cash register.

For serial shoppers, reduced prices have an appeal beyond the bustle and brightness of the
10 shop – they are a shopper's little pain-killer. Worried that your spending is beyond control? Stick to the bargains and they ease any uncomfortable feelings running through your head about wasting your money on things which you do not really need. You can even indulge in some smugness: others pay high amounts; you open your wallet only when the prices get lower.

15 The bad news is that you are not as smart as you think. The shop will make a profit whether its items are reduced or not: its "SALE" just reduces the amount of profit it makes. They are still after your money but just less of it. On a busy bargain-hunt, drawn in by the shop's lure, how many of us have unexpectedly bought items that were not in the sale at all? They capture your cash in many ways.

20 Shops are really like the nets fishermen have put over the side of their boats for centuries: they get us in, get us over the door and we are caught like wriggling fish: you came into the place for new trousers; you left with a shirt and a belt you liked to go with them. Clever little places shops, when you think about it. But then they need to be clever if they are planning to stay open, pay their staff, their business rates and all the rest of it.

25 I was above all of that, able to see all the little tricks shops use, until I went to the sales myself recently. It was a little quieter than I expected but all the reductions, the "price blitz", the "amazing deals", the "unbelievable prices" just pulled me out of the cold and over the door. On a shelf about chest height sat a lovely pair of burgundy shoes. They were a size above mine but their leather soles were untarnished by our grubby streets, had a lovely smell
30 and shone like a well-rubbed cricket ball. At "half-price" there was no need to try them on – at that price you pounce! There are, after all, plenty of other bargain hunters behind you, happy to grab anything you pass over. The shoes, fit for a captain of industry, fit for a lord of the manor, were mine!

At the counter I learned that all products were reduced by a further twenty per cent for "one
35 day only". I was on a roll! This is how hunters would have felt thousands of years ago when their well-aimed arrow killed two beasts at once. I was a trawler man with a full net. Shop assistants, however, do not discuss hunting or fishing with you; they ask if you "need a bag". I declined the offer of anything to put them in and under my arm my shining shoes were tucked.

40 Time was when products taken from a shop this way would have attracted the attention of security, but these days bags are for first-class customers who pay a little extra. I was in bag-free economy class, spending just what they asked and no more. Who needs a bag anyway when you get a bargain and your grin covers a significant percentage of your face?

I sat them on the passenger seat of the car for the journey home – that waft of leathery odour
45 dispelling some of the vehicle's usual pongs. The original price tag of £150 was a week's wages just thirty years ago but my price £75, less 20 per cent, made these a luxury without the unsettling price tag. I would never do that crazy thing where they camp outside the shop overnight and then rush the doors on the first day of the sale. You get on a lifeboat like that, you exit a burning building at that pace but you do not race towards a pile of reduced clothes
50 or a half-price coffee maker in that way. I like to preserve my dignity; I don't need the sleeping bag at the door and a television crew filming it all; I follow the sale signs and buy shoes at a price so low my parents would have been comfortable with it.

The shops most days secretly hope for a stampede of buyers but have to settle for a trickle of purchases. I had been in the trickle and happy about it until an uncomfortable thought came
55 to me: perhaps I had just bought the type of footwear no one else wanted? I already have more shoes than I can wear. A psychologist would have things to say about that but you don't speak to a psychologist at the sales.

At the traffic lights on the drive home, I observed a woman old enough to be a grandmother.

Behind her was her grandson. He was pulling a four-wheeled trolley with a second-hand
60 fridge placed on it. Their fridge needed cleaning but it looked as if their journey would end with the appliance being installed in granny's kitchen. My shopping was solitary; the old woman clearly had an assistant she could be proud of. With the lights holding back my car they crossed the road. Gran was obviously pleased with her purchase; her grandson seemed pleased to be helping her. I had shopped for shoes I would probably not wear; granny had a
65 "new" fridge she could rely on for a while. When it comes to bargains, she could have shown me a thing or two.

James Getty

Questions – Hunting for Bargains is Complicated

1. Using your **own words** give two examples of what *"reluctant spenders"*, lines 2 – 5, prefer to do. (2 marks)
2. How does the writer's **word choice,** lines 6 – 8, convey that the shops have a lot of stock to sell at the sale? (2 marks)
3. How does the writer's **imagery**, lines 9 – 10, convey how welcome *"reduced prices"* are for those who shop regularly? (3 marks)
4. Using your **own words**, refer to lines 12 – 14 and explain why bargain hunters feel *"some smugness"*. (2 marks)
5. Using your **own words** as far as possible read lines 15 – 17 and explain what the writer feels is the *"bad news"* about sales. (2 marks)
6. Give **two examples** of how the **writer's language**, lines 17 – 19, conveys the power of shops and a shopper's attraction to them. (4 marks)
7. How does one example of the writer's **imagery**, lines 20 – 24, show how "clever" shops are when they attract customers? (3 marks)
8. Using your **own words**, explain why, according to the writer, lines 23 – 24, shops *"need to be clever"*. (2 marks)
9. How do lines 25 – 26, act as a **link** at this stage in the passage? (2 marks)
10. Choose **either word-choice or imagery**, lines 28-30, and then explain why it conveys the writer's attraction to the shoes. (2 marks)
11. In lines 32 – 33 what **tone** does the writer convey at this point in the passage? (1 mark)
12. Read lines 47 – 51 and using **your own words** explain what the writer would *"never do"* before a sale began. (2 marks)
13. How do at least three examples of the writer's **word choice,** lines 60 – 66, create an effective ending to the passage? (3 marks)

30 marks

Answers – Hunting for Bargains is Complicated

1. *Pupils must use their own words as far as possible. Complete quotations = zero marks. One mark for any of the following:*

- Watching sport
- Taking part in climbing
- Enjoying the outdoors

2. *One mark for quotation of word and one mark for appropriate explanation.*

- "piled" – conveys the vastness of the shop's stock
- "pyramid-high" – suggests the large amounts of stock

3. *One mark for quotation / identification of image and one mark for explanation.*

- "pain-killer" – suggests that shopping brings happiness and comfort and can make a person feel satisfied

4. *Pupils must use their own words as far as possible. Complete quotations = zero marks. One mark for any of the following:*

- Other people spend lots of money
- They spend less; others are lavish
- Bargain hunters are clever

5. *Pupils must use their own words as far as possible. Complete quotations = zero marks. One mark for any of the following:*

- The shop is still making money, just not as much
- Shop continues to cost you money just not as much as normal

6. *One mark for identification of language technique and one mark for appropriate explanation.*

Language technique:

- "busy bargain hunt" – alliteration conveys the activity around reduced prices
- "capture your cash" – alliteration conveys just how effective shops can be in enticing shoppers

Imagery:

- "the shop's lure" – metaphor conveys just how attractive shops are to some people

7. *One mark for quotation / identification of image and one mark for explanation.*

- "like the nets fishermen have" – suggests that shops can be difficult to leave and attract shoppers in / catch them unaware / create a trap etc.

- "we are caught like wriggling fish" – suggests that shoppers are brought into a shop and encouraged to spend / have few alternatives / are manipulated etc.

8. *Pupils must use their own words as far as possible. Complete quotations = zero marks. One mark for any of the following:*

- They need to encourage spending to stay in business
- Stop themselves from going bust
- Remain trading
- Remain able to pay salaries/money to staff
- Pay their rent/expenses

9. *Pupils need only identify one side of the link for full marks – one mark for quotation and one mark for identification.*

- "I was above all of that…" – links back to the way shops get you to spend money
- "…until I went to the sales myself recently" – links forward and introduces the writer's trip to buy his shoes

10. *One mark for quotation / identification of techniques and one more for explanation.*

Word choice

- "lovely pair" – suggests attraction
- "leather soles untarnished" – suggests how new they looked
- "lovely smell" – suggests attractive aroma
- "…and shone" – suggests how bright/attractive they were

Imagery

- "shone like a well-rubbed cricket ball" – highlights that shoes are appealing to look at and they can be attractive / eye-catching etc.

11. *One mark for identification of tone.*

Possible tones:

- Happy
- Euphoric
- Overjoyed
- Light-hearted
- Pleased with himself

12. *Pupils must use their own words as far as possible. Complete quotations = zero marks. One mark for any of the following:*

- He would not sit at the door of a sale waiting for the opening.

- He would not run to the entrance at opening time.
- He would not sleep at the shop to be at the head of the queue
- He would not have the media record it all

13. *One mark for quotation of word and one mark for appropriate explanation.*

- "the appliance…installed in granny's kitchen" – suggests it will be useful
- "my shopping was solitary" – suggests the writer is alone
- "…an assistant she could be proud of" – suggests she is proud of her grandson
- "gran was obviously pleased" – suggests her delight with the fridge
- "…pleased to be helping her" – suggests the boy likes to be useful
- "…shoes…I probably would not wear" – suggests the writer's doubts about his bargain
- "granny had a new fridge she could rely on" – suggests her delight
- "…could have shown me a thing or two" – suggests the lady knows how to buy things you need inexpensively.

Pupils and Potatoes: how gardens enrich education

In this article the author discusses the importance of gardening to secondary education. He writes about his experience of building a garden and the benefits and difficulties he faced.

"What are those?" one of my pupils asked me.

I looked over at two large raised beds. A warm autumn sun was falling on the school garden. "Those are potatoes," I answered.

The pupil in front of me was a nice girl called Jennifer. In class she usually had her head
5 down, focused on the work in front of her. Today, however, her face was furrowed as she looked over at the raised beds.

"But…" she began. Her voice trailed off as she took a few steps toward the plants. With a sinking feeling I knew where this conversation was going.

Jennifer started again, "But they're green. Aren't potatoes brown?"

10 I nodded. "Well, the bits we eat, the roots, are brown. What you're looking at is the part above the soil. That's what all those leaves are." I tried my hardest not to sound patronising.

Jennifer looked baffled. She shook her head and just said, "Hmm."

I knew that the situation called for drastic action. I reached over to the potato plant, grabbed it by its green foliage, and pulled. As the plant was raised into the air, several large tubers
15 dropped onto the compost. I held the plant aloft, showing off a few more potatoes that were still attached at the roots. I think the variety we planted that year was 'Kestrel'. They were good potatoes. I was happy with them.

Jennifer, on the other hand, stood with a shocked look on her face. It was an expression somewhere between disgust and horror. It was as if I had just done something terrible. I'd
20 killed the plant. She took a few steps back. I tried to reassure her, "Jennifer, it's okay. You have to dig up the plant to get the potatoes. Look." I held one out for her to touch.

As she took the potato in her hand, understanding began to spread across her face. Once removed from the stems and leaves, the tuber was now something she recognised. She looked at me and smiled. It was a genuine smile and she simply said, "I had no idea that this is where
25 they came from."

For me, that pretty much sums up how much young people seem to know these days about their food and its production. And as for any wider understanding of horticulture – forget it.

This is why I started an eco-garden at my secondary school a few years ago. It was a difficult project to get started and has been difficult to maintain. However, it has been truly rewarding. When I first approached my school about building a garden I was told, “Oh yeah, a few people have tried that. No one seems to have had any success.” There had been a small sliver of land set aside for a garden when the school was built, but except for a dead apple tree someone had stuck in the boggy ground some time ago, nothing had been developed. It was just a neglected area of weedy grass.

The first thing I did was to ask the school if there was any money available to kick-start the garden. They looked at me as if I had just asked to take my pupils free-climbing over a gorge of broken glass and pit vipers. The senior management’s faces said no before their mouths even opened. There is an unspoken rule about most requests for money in any secondary school: if your request does not involve raising attainment (exam results), then it’s probably best not to ask. Unfortunately, there is no exam which requires pupils to identify a foxglove from a cornflower, and therefore gardening is about as popular with most head teachers as showing DVDs on a Monday morning. We just don’t do that type of thing; not if you want to keep your job.

I quickly realised that the money would have to come from somewhere else. I looked online and found that there was funding available through several charities. I applied to Awards for All, which is funded through the Big Lottery Fund. I filled in the forms and mailed them off. I waited. I crossed my fingers. A short time later I received a reply. Their answer was, yes. I was able to secure enough money to dig out part of the garden, put in paths and a seating area, build a few raised beds, and buy a few plants. It was a start.

To the school’s credit, once they found out I had secured some funding they did find a little money to build a shed and purchase some tools for the pupils. I’ve always found that once momentum gathers behind a project, more and more people are willing to jump on board. When a small digger rolled in to start excavating out the compacted clay soil, people took notice.

Since then we’ve had some real successes and some minor failures. Despite any setbacks, developing the school garden has been extraordinarily rewarding. It is a space which helps to connect pupils to the natural world. Interacting with nature teaches young people more than most textbooks. Something as simple as a garden can open up questions about both science and philosophy – show me a worksheet that is able to do that. In short, every subject can find beneficial links to gardening and horticulture.

Remembering that day and the look of shock and amazement on Jennifer’s face about something as simple as a potato was a wonderful experience. We need pupils to be given more opportunities to learn about horticulture and interact with nature. Schools need to realise that just because something can’t be quantified and stuck on a spreadsheet, doesn’t mean it isn’t important.

Education is about more than exam results. What should matter most in education is inspiring young people to be critical of the world around them, to actively engage with knowledge, and to ask questions about their environment – even if that question is about something as simple as where a potato comes from.

Tom Smart – originally published in The Guardian

Questions – Pupils and Potatoes

1. In lines 4 – 12, how does the **language** make clear the pupil's (Jennifer) confusion when the teacher tries to explain how potatoes grow? (4 Marks)
2. Read lines 13 – 17. **In your own words**, what does the author do in order demonstrate the way in which a potato grows? (2 marks)
3. How does the **word choice** in lines 18 – 21 help to make clear that the pupil finds the author's actions unexpected? (2 marks)
4. **Summarise** Jennifer's reaction (lines 18 – 21) to finding out how a potato grows. (2 marks)
5. How does the **sentence structure** in lines 26-27 help to emphasize that most secondary pupils know very little about how plants grow? (2 marks)
6. How does line 28 help to create a **link** in the article? (2 marks)
7. What is the author's **tone** in line 35 – 37? How does the **language** help to make the author's tone clear? (2 marks)
8. Read lines 38 – 43. **In your own words**, explain the school's reaction to the author wanting to build an eco-garden? (2 marks)
9. How does the **sentence structure** in lines 45 – 47 help to make clear that the author was anxious about applying for money to build and eco-garden? (2marks)
10. How does the **language** in lines 48 – 49 emphasize that the garden got off to a positive start? (2 marks)
11. How does the **word choice** in line 55 – 57 help to highlight the author's view that developing an eco-garden has been a good experience? (2 marks)
12. **In your own words**, according to lines 55 – 60, summaries the benefits of an eco-garden to education. (3 marks)
13. Read lines 63 – 66. **Summarise** one criticism of secondary schools the author expresses. (1 mark)
14. How is the last sentence, lines 66 – 69, an effective conclusion to the article as a whole. You may comment on **ideas** or **language** in your answer. (2 marks)

30 marks

Answers – "Pupils and Potatoes"

1. *One mark for quotation / identification of techniques and one more for explanation.*

   Word Choice

   - "furrowed" – suggests serious concentration and therefore a need for understanding
   - "baffled" – suggests that Jennifer lacks the knowledge necessary to understand how plants grow

   Imagery

   - "furrowed" – comparison of the girl's face to a ploughed field; helps to highlight that Jennifer must be working hard to comprehend the situation

   Sentence Structure

   - "But…" – the dialogue and ellipsis help to highlight that the pupil is confused as to the process of potato growing
   - "Aren't potatoes brown?" – the question helps to indicate that Jennifer obviously does not understand how potatoes grow

2. *Pupils must use their own words as far as possible. Complete quotations = zero marks. One mark for any of the following:*

   - The author grabs hold of the potato plant and pulls it from the ground
   - The author shows the tubers (potatoes) to the pupil

3. *One mark for quotation / identification of word and one more for explanation.*

   - "shocked" – suggests that Jennifer did not expect the plant to be torn from the ground
   - "disgust" – suggests that the pupil did not like to see the plant destroyed
   - "horror" – suggests that Jennifer found digging up the plant disturbing and frightening
   - "terrible" – suggests that the pupil did not find the experience pleasant

4. *Pupils must use their own words as far as possible. Complete quotations = zero marks. One mark for any of the following:*

   - Jennifer is surprised / shaken by seeing the potato plant taken from the ground

- She seems to have the opinion that the author has done something reprehensible or wrong

5. *One mark for identification of sentence structure and one mark for explanation.*

    - "…wider understanding of horticulture – forget it." – the author's use of a dash helps to create a pause and emphasize his key point that few young people understand the importance of, or how to, grow plants

6. *Pupils need only identify how the sentence links forward OR backward for full marks. One mark for quotation and one mark for appropriate explanation.*

    - "This is why…" – this links back to the author's opinion that few young people know or care about how plants grow
    - "…started an eco-garden" – links forward to the author's attempt to build an eco-garden at a high school in order to further engage pupils in growing plants

7. *One mark for identification of tone. One mark for how the tone is created.*

    - The author's tone is humorous / tongue-in-cheek

    - "free-climbing over a gorge of broken glass and pit vipers" – the exaggerated image helps to highlight the response the author received when asking for funding / money; the hyperbole creates a humorous tone

8. *Pupils must use their own words as far as possible. Complete quotations = zero marks. One mark for any of the following:*

    - The school was not able / willing to supply the author with the funding he desired
    - The school was more interested in test results than building a garden
    - The school did not see the value in an eco-garden

9. *One mark for a quotation of sentence structure and one mark for explanation.*

    - Use of short sentence "I waited." – the author's use of a short sentence helps to create tension and emphasizes his apprehension about a possible rejection of the funding for the school garden
    - Paragraph builds to a climax "I looked online and found that there was funding… Their answer was, yes." – the paragraph builds to the climax about funding becoming available for the garden, which highlights the author's nervousness

- Repetition of sentence pattern starting with "I" – helps to focus attention on the author's feelings of worry

10. *One mark for quotation / identification of techniques and one more for explanation.*

Sentence structure

- The use of a list "...dig out part of the garden, put in paths and a seating area, build a few..." – the list helps to emphasize the number of things the author was able to accomplish, therefore making the start of the garden a success
- Short sentence "It was a start." – simple upbeat statement about the beginnings of the garden; helps to highlight the optimistic start

11. *One mark for quotation / identification of word and one more for explanation.*

- "successes" – suggests that the garden has been a benefit to the school / the author enjoyed the garden
- "extraordinarily rewarding" – suggests that the garden and its creation was a positive experience for the staff and pupils

12. *Pupils must use their own words as far as possible. Complete quotations = zero marks. One mark for any of the following:*

- Pupils are able to interact with nature / plants / living things
- Gardening can help pupils to ask questions / make links to new ideas
- Gardening is more engaging than traditional teaching approaches – "worksheets"
- Many subjects can find relevant aspects / ways to use or connect their curriculum to gardening

13. *Pupils must use their own words as far as possible. Complete quotations = zero marks. One mark for any of the following:*

- High schools are too interested in things they can measure
- Schools are too exam-driven / focused on tests
- Learning which can't be tested should still be valued

14. *Question should be marked on merit. One mark for a basic comment on ideas or techniques and two marks for a more in-depth analysis.*

Possible comments may include:

- Simple declarative statement "Education is about more than exam results." – effectively summarises one of the author's belief in inventive teaching methods, such as an eco-garden

- Use of a list of aspirational goals "…matter most in education is inspiring young people to be critical of the world around them, to actively engage with knowledge…" – helps to highlight all of the things an eco-garden can provide to a school
- Use of a dash "…ask questions about their environment – even if that question is about something as simple as where a potato comes from." – helps to emphasize the author's view that learning about the natural world is important
- Humorous tone which connects to the title of the article "something as simple as where a potato comes from."

Across the Great Divide

On a visit to Hadrian's Wall in Northumberland, the writer discovers, to his surprise, that the Roman's famous barrier may have had a complicated history.

The girl we met at breakfast in the hotel that morning was an enthusiastic New Zealander, enjoying, she said, a Britain full of history. In New Zealand, she explained, they put special plaques on houses which were built a hundred years ago. In a country so newly-developed, these dwellings are something of a landmark to come and stare at. Judging by what she had 5 seen so far, she had calculated that the men who put the plaques up on the "ancient" buildings in New Zealand, would be swamped with business in Britain.

On holiday in what the brochure calls "Hadrian's Wall Country", we enjoyed an encounter with history too. We were not as new to it as our friend from the other side of the world, but the photographs of the wall we once studied seemed poor in comparison to the actual 10 construction itself. As you survey the ruin, and think about the massive effort to build it, there is a sense of awe.

You appreciate the enormity of the task the Romans undertook when they built a barrier from Carlisle to the Newcastle, involving 80 miles of carefully placed stones and defensive ditches; and, of course, a Roman road, behind the wall, straight as a well-planned motorway, 15 from one side of the country to the other. In a time before diggers, truck and cranes – construction commenced in AD122 – it was a job for a lot of strong and hardy builders.

At the preserved site of Housesteads, ten miles from the nearest town of Corbridge, the wall and an adjoining fort are built on such high ground that even a walker, carrying no more than a mobile phone, arrives breathless and panting. Someone once had to carry stones up here 20 and then start building!

At sites like this, and others, such as the stretch of wall along Peel Crag, four miles from Housesteads, the briefest of visits confirms the Roman's legendary building skills. These boys were confidently cutting the country in two by placing one rock on top of another for as far as the eye can see. Yet while you can't help but be amazed at their hard work over long 25 hours, in all types of weather, you can feel a sense of sadness about the pointlessness of the whole project.

You see dividing a country in half artificially is always a temporary measure. It never lasts. The patterns and events of history tell you that. Perhaps only the arrogance of Roman leaders, believing their empire was forever, could have made them think otherwise. They did not have 30 history books anyway and the project went ahead, using any stones available for miles around.

Did morale among the Roman soldiers and their assistants sink to their boots, made worse by the widespread miseries with which soldiers of every age have had to work in? You wonder what the grumbles and groans, passed from one man to another, would have been like. Or did 35 they realise that they were creating an amazing tourist attraction that would outlive them all?

The chances are that no words would have been exchanged on the matter by Romans at all.
Many of the garrisons that once lived and worked here were made from a variety of
Europeans, people who had simply joined the ranks of the Roman Empire and followed
orders. Housteads, for example, was maintained and guarded by the first cohort of
40 "Tungrains", a regiment raised in modern Belgium. The Empire diversified.

So Europeans, other than Romans were here, but what is startling is the knowledge that some
young Englishmen may have joined the ranks of the Empire too. Excavations on the Rhine
revealed the presence at one time of British troops, known as "Brittones" and serving Rome
in its German territories. "Romans" were not just soldiers from Italy.

45 Another surprise emerges when you study the wall's original height. At about five metres it
was too low to prevent a determined army crossing it. The wall may have been too lightly
manned to muster a proper defence. Each fort along its length was only large enough to house
and sustain around thirty troops.

So if it was too low and did not have enough soldiers then a theory that it was just the official
50 boundary mark of the Roman Empire becomes believable. Could it have been there partly to
check and observe who came through it and charge a fee for doing so? This seems likely. To
the north of the wall, remember, lay Caledonian, modern Scotland, an area never fully
occupied by the Romans.

This boundary function would have declined from time to time. The Romans were busy and
55 liked to travel. In AD 139 a second wall was built, this time in Scotland, between the river
Clyde and the Forth. Under orders from Hadrian's successor, Antonius Pius, Scotland was to
be part of the Empire too. In historical terms this plan was brief and by AD160, the Scottish
wall, a smaller fish, at only forty miles long, was abandoned. The reasons for leaving
Scotland are mysterious but hostility from local tribes is a possibility. A general lack of
60 troops to occupy and monitor two walls may have been another reason. Hadrian's Wall was
back in business, the official "border" again.

The following years, AD300-340, were a time of peace and ordinary activity. However, the
wall had been in place and working for two hundred years when, in AD360, it was the victim
of what may have been a serious attack by a group of local tribes. This may not have been the
65 only time the wall had been formally challenged and the Romans, after extensive repair work
and perhaps some reinforcements, had it up and running again, under their control. Who
knows what happened to the attacking tribes?

In their time the Romans did have an impressive development programme: two significant
walls, a complex system of straight roads and several large towns. That says something about
70 their industriousness and something about the uncompromising nature of occupying armies.
All of these developments may have pushed the locals around or out of the way.

We can only guess from the distance of two thousand years how public opinion reacted to all
of this. Did the Romans encounter jeering, protesting crowds every time they marched a
legion here or there; or were people just bewildered and intimidated by a large army? The

75 history books suggest the latter. Romans were intimidating and resisting them took a strong stomach so it may have been wise simply to go along with it all.

Yet for all of its apparent power and control, the occupation of the area was only to last another forty years. In AD400, the wall was abandoned. Ruling Britain had been judged a luxury by the high command and the soldiers here were put elsewhere to defend other areas
80 of Roman territory. The wall was left slowly to decline. Building a house, a bridge or a road yourself? There were no Romans around and you could get lots of finely cut stones free from their wall for your project. In some places, after a few decades, only crumbling foundations were left to mark the original construction.

The talkative girl from New Zealand was going to see the wall that morning, then take the
85 road south. Like the Romans her stay was short and heading back home was what she would do when, just like them, her resources ran out.

James Getty – Originally published in The Yorkshire Post

Questions – Across the Great Divide

1. Using your **own words**, explain how old buildings (lines 1 – 6) are recognised in New Zealand. (2 marks)
2. Re-read lines 1 – 4.

   How does **word choice** convey that the girl's feelings about her trip to Britain? (2 marks)
3. How does the **imagery** in lines 14 – 15 suggest that the Roman road was an effective one? (2 marks)
4. How does **word choice**, paragraph four, lines 17 – 20 suggest that the fort was high up? (2 marks)
5. In lines 21 – 24 identify the **tone** the writer uses and how it is created. *"These boys were confidently cutting the country in two... "?* (2 marks)
6. Read lines 27 – 31.

   Explain, using your **own words**, what Roman leaders believed about their project. (2 marks)
7. Read line 36.

   How does the sentence beginning "Chances are…" act as an effective **link**? (2 marks)
8. Read lines 36 – 40.

   Using your **own words**, explain three points the author makes about the way the Roman army was made up? (3 marks)
9. Using your **own words**, explain what evidence the author has in for claiming the wall was "lightly manned", lines 45 – 48. (2 marks)
10. In lines 49-53, what does the author claim the wall was for? Please **use your own words** in your explanation. (2 marks)
11. How does the author use **imagery,** lines 57 – 59, to suggest the Scottish wall was a much smaller version of Hadrian's Wall? (2 marks)
12. In lines 72 – 76, use **your own words to** explain how the author thinks local people would have reacted to the Romans. (2 marks)
13. In lines 77 – 83, how does the author's **word choice** suggest what became of the wall when the Romans left? (2 marks)
14. How **effective** do you think the final paragraph is at ending the passage? (3 marks)

30 Marks

Answers – Across the Great Divide

1. *Pupils must use their own words as far as possible. Complete quotations = zero marks. One mark for any of the following:*

    - They put little signs / notices / on them
    - Saying they are old

2. *One mark for quotation of word and one mark for appropriate explanation.*

    - "enthusiastic" – suggests she was full of cheerfulness etc.
    - "enjoying" – suggests she liked her time in Britain doing history.

3. *One mark for a quotation / identification of image and one mark for explanation.*

    - "…straight as a well-planned motorway" – helps to highlight that the road was not curved; both allowed movement and travel and they can exist for long periods/could be a route of transport for long periods.

4. *One mark for quotation of word and one mark for appropriate explanation.*

    - "breathless" suggests such an effort you are out of breath getting there
    - "panting" suggests that tiredness and fatigue result when getting there

5. *One for identification of tone, one mark for how the tone is created. Possible tones include:*
    - informal
    - light-hearted
    - humorous

    Tone is created by any of the following:

    - cutting…country" – hyperbole or exaggeration:"
    - "cutting…country in two" – alliterative language:
    - Comment on the humorous image of cutting the country in half
    - "These boys…" – informal language

6. *Pupils must use their own words as far as possible. Complete quotations = zero marks. One mark for any of the following:*

    - They believed it would always be there
    - It would last for ages
    - Was worth doing, etc.

7. *Pupils need only identify how the sentence links forward OR backward for full marks. One mark for quotation and one mark for appropriate explanation.*

- The phrase: "The chances are that no words would have been exchanged..." returns to idea of soldiers moaning about their life; the phrase: "...by Romans at all" introduces the idea that the actual soldiers came from several European countries, including Belgium.

8. *Pupils must use their own words as far as possible. Complete quotations = zero marks. One mark for any of the following:*

- It was made up with soldiers from various nations
- Some soldiers were happy to join a powerful army
- Romans were not just from Rome

9. *Pupils must use their own words as far as possible. Complete quotations = zero marks. One mark for any of the following:*

- The forts on the wall could only hold small numbers of soldiers.
- The forts could not protect or maintain many troops

10. *Pupils must use their own words as far as possible. Complete quotations = zero marks. One mark for any of the following:*
- A border crossing
- A place to observe the area from
- A place to take tolls / money from people passing through

11. *One mark for identification of image and one mark for appropriate explanation.*

- "a smaller fish" metaphor
- Like a smaller fish, the Scottish wall was not as important or prized as Hadrian's; both small fishes and small walls are given up/abandoned quickly; they can be disappointing, not effective...etc

12. *Pupils must use their own words as far as possible. Complete quotations = zero marks. One mark for any of the following:*

- They would have been scared/kept quiet
- Locals just got on with things mostly
- They thought that accepting was the best way to stay safe
- They would have been wary of a big army.

13. One mark for quotation / identification of word and one more for explanation.

- "abandoned" suggests left alone with no one to care for it
- "judged a luxury" suggests they thought they no longer need it
- "decline" suggests it slowly gets worse, falls apart
- "crumbling" suggests it is turning to fragments from once being powerful

14. Effective: Any two points, well explained, could gain up to three marks

- she is compared to the Romans, staying for a short time, then going south
- her resources like theirs were limited and eventually both return to their own country
- marks could be awarded for recognising use of parenthesis "just like them" as link between the Romans as travellers and the girl.

30 marks

Tattoos

In this passage the writer thinks that tattoos will probably always be popular, but decides that they are not for him.

Bruce, two doors down from us, joined the army after leaving school. He had been a shy youth but was always polite to adults; he weeded his mother's garden in the school holidays. Six months later, having joined-up, he spent his leave in the pub saying hello to everyone again. His short-sleeved shirt revealed two huge tattoos on his arms, each the length of a hair-dryer nozzle. In a quiet town his inky adornment was greeted with widespread shock, for people knew that the meeting of needles and ink on his skin created a mark for life. Bruce had joined a regiment full of men trained to point guns and crawl on the ground; men sent where the politicians created wars; men who liked to grunt and sweat and run for miles in heavy boots. For them, what better a badge of manhood than the tattoo?

Tattoos, like motorbikes are edgy; the ink from the tip of a pin helps put you with the cool guys. Exclusions from school and jeans with more holes than material are for rebellious youths; tattoos are for men. They are great for young soldiers and even better for touring rock stars. On stage, like chunky jewellery or chest hair, the tattoo is a lure for fans' eyes. During an encore, reduced to your vest, the exposed ink on the skin adds to a rock star's credibility. Sometimes, however, skin adornments have only to be exposed on stage as even rock stars have disapproving mothers and grandmothers who worry that Rick or Harry with the recording contract and fans, have been to the shop with the buzzing needles and had a "horrible" tattoo spoil their lovely skin forever.

In the boardroom they are simply not acceptable and everywhere would-be executives buy double-cuffed shirts to cover the things up. They were a good idea ten years ago when you were in a band or about to design surfboards for a living but one glimpse of them in a professional meeting and your reputation with other business leaders shrinks. Unlike your tattoo, of course, which, in some lights, if you are not careful, will shine embarrassingly through slim-fit white shirts.

But away from the modern army, away from the business world, there was always something gloomy about old men's tattoos. They told a different story. My uncles were quiet men with firm jaw lines and tobacco tins the size of instant cameras; their tattoos looked like drawings someone had tried to rub out and they helped to destroy the myth that the ink and the needle last. For the fact is that even the best ones change colour with time. Those inky lines started somewhere between navy and royal blue in colour but, with the years, they turned into something close to the colour of faded jeans and when the tattoo turns pale, injecting fresh ink is impossible.

In the uncles' brash youth, victims of peer pressure and sometimes fuelled with drink, they ended up outside the buzzing tattoo booths and the trip from the door to the chair and needles was a kind of dare. Oh, it was sore at the time and, like an inky form of sunburn, tender for days afterwards. But everyone was doing it and within a crowd even stupid things can somehow seem like fun that does no harm.

The uncles had all done national-service: a time after the Second World War when everyone had to serve some time in the armed forces. It had been a macho military world, far from
40 home, and somehow the tattoo helped you bond with the mixed bunch of people they shaped into a regiment. In a male-dominated culture others could not admire your haircut or the new shoes you bought to go on leave, but they could gaze at your tattoo; they would gather like art students around an important painting. Even if they disliked it, the fact that you had been brave enough to face the tattoo needles gave you a little inch of street credibility in a culture
45 where all of that mattered.

But a sad creature is the thirty-year-old tattoo. It is the colour of a varicose vein*.

In some unfortunate cases the tattoo's ink runs parallel to the wrinkled skin and the look is terrible. From five yards you cannot tell what an old tattoo was once meant to be. You might spot a star or a heart shape but the "body" of a mediocre ageing tattoo reduces to a splodge of
50 unattractive marks that spread under the skin. In the 1950s and 1960s, very little tattoo work was regulated. The skilled tattoo artist knew what his steady hand was doing; separating him from the needle-happy twitching novice was difficult until years later when, shirtless, a look in the mirror told you the truth: the tattoo you once displayed in the barracks was now a terrible mess.

55 Yet all of that is not talked about in today's tattoo market. Men and women in the last ten or fifteen years have kept the demand for these skin paintings alive. Most tattoo parlours are booked weeks in advance; people fall over themselves to get in the door. The modern man goes further than the old uncles: his tattoo adornments start at the wrist and end at the shoulder. From a distance on a beach they look like patchy arm stockings. But fashion has
60 what it wants and the only "too-far" look these days is the face. You can get a tattoo anywhere but there, most people seem to think. A star on the neck is fashionable in some situations but facial ink remains the choice of the hardcore tattoo wearer.

In my book it is all a bit different: life brings enough ready-made problems and the bright tattoo I get today will simply not stay that way. Fading images on the skin are enough to
65 scare me off; for others, they may be part of the attraction – why not grow old with the marks of your choice, I can hear them say. The cautious, however, will denounce tattoos as a risky game: fashionable today, they might be old-fashioned and ridiculous in the future. In spite of all of that, until they are linked to a serious illness, it looks as if we, like Bruce at the start of this story, will pay to have ink squirted under our skin.

*varicose vein – a big blood vessel in your skin that sticks out unattractively.

James Getty

Questions – Tattoos

1. Look at lines 1 – 3. Using your **own words** explain two things about Bruce's personality before he joined the army. (2 marks)
2. Look at lines 3 – 7 and explain, using your **own words** two reasons why people in the town were shocked by his tattoos. (2 marks)
3. Look at lines 7 – 10. How does the writer's **word choice** help explain what the men in the army were like? You should find two examples and explain them. (4 marks)
4. Look at lines 13 – 17. Using your **own words** explain two reasons why "rock stars" like tattoos. (2 marks)
5. Look at lines 19 – 24. How does the writer's **word choice** convey what "business leaders" feel about tattoos? (2 marks)
6. Look at lines 25 – 28. How does the writer's **imagery** convey what he thinks about old tattoos? (2 marks)
7. Look at lines 33 – 36. Using your **own words** explain two things that persuaded the uncles to get tattoos. (2 marks)
8. Look at lines 41 – 43. How does the writer use **imagery** to convey the importance of the tattoo to other soldiers? (2 marks)
9. Look at lines 46 –50. How does one example of the writer's **word choice** convey his feelings about old tattoos? (2 marks)
10. Look at lines 50 – 54. How does the writer's **sentence structure** and **word choice** make clear that not all tattoo artists are the same? (4 marks)
11. How does line 55 act as a **link** at this point in the passage? (2 marks)
12. Look at lines 56 – 58. How does the writer's **word choice** convey the popularity of tattoos today? (2 marks)
13. Look at line 63 until the end of the passage. **Explain** why this makes a suitable conclusion to the passage. (2 marks)

30 marks

Answers – Tattoos

1. *Pupils must use their own words as far as possible. Complete quotations = zero marks. One mark for any of the following:*

    - He lacked confidence
    - He was quiet
    - Was helpful to his mother
    - He was polite to people older than him

2. *Pupils must use their own words as far as possible. Complete quotations = zero marks. One mark for any of the following:*

    - His tattoos were big
    - In this place people did not do that
    - The tattoos were for ever
    - They could not be removed

3. *One mark for quotation and one mark for appropriate explanation.*

    - "trained to point guns" – suggests they are serious soldiers, able to kill
    - "...crawl on the ground" – suggests they are used to rough training
    - "...sent where the politicians created wars" – suggests they are men who are used to being sent to terrible/dangerous places/to battles etc.
    - "grunt and sweat and run for miles in heavy boots" – suggests they are fit and tough and well trained etc

4. *Pupils must use their own words as far as possible. Complete quotations = zero marks. One mark for any of the following:*

    - They are great for getting the attention of your admirers
    - They look great on stage when you take some of your clothes off
    - They make you look like a real celebrity

5. *One mark for quotation and one mark for appropriate explanation.*

    - "...simply not acceptable" – suggests they do not tolerate them or find them attractive etc
    - "...to cover the things up" – suggests it is best to wear clothes that do not expose them
    - "...your reputation with other business leaders shrinks" – suggests that tattoos make you an outsider/not like the other important people etc.

6. *One mark for quotation / identification of image and one mark for explanation.*

.

- "…tattoos looked like drawings someone had tried to rub out": simile
- Just as a rubbed out drawing is messy or unattractive, so too is a tattoo; both are hard to see properly and they can be embarrassing/not something you want other people to see.

7. *Pupils must use their own words as far as possible. Complete quotations = zero marks. One mark for any of the following:*

- They were influenced by friends
- They had drunk alcohol
- They challenged each other to do it

8. *One mark for quotation / identification of image and one mark for explanation.*

.

- "…like art students around an important painting" simile
- Just as students take an interest in art, the other soldiers examined the tattoo; both students and soldiers admire what they are looking at and they can study/ discuss for some time

9. *One mark for quotation and one mark for appropriate explanation.*

- "sad creature" metaphor compares it to a sad animal
- "colour of a varicose vein" suggests it looks horrible
- "runs parallel to wrinkled skin" suggests a dreadful appearance
- "the look is terrible" suggests a complete rejection

10. *One mark for identification of technique and one mark for an appropriate explanation.*

Sentence structure:

- The "skilled tattoo artist…" contrasts with the "needle-happy novice
- or/
- "…a look in the mirror" makes a statement separated by a colon, then an explanation of the "mess" a tattoo has become

Word choice:

- "skilled tattoo artist" suggests he knows what he is doing; contrasts with "needle-happy" which suggests he is unskilled with his equipment

or/

- "steady hand" suggests he was accurate/confident; contrasts with "twitching novice" which suggests he is unsteady and inexperienced

11. *Pupils must identify how the sentence either links forward or backward. One mark for quotation and one mark for explanation.*

The phrase: "Yet all of that…" returns to the idea of old tattoos, sometimes done badly; the phrase: "…in today's tattoo market" introduces the large amount/demand for tattoos today.

12. *One good selection with an explanation for two marks.*

Any one of:

- "demand…alive" suggests they are very popular
- "booked weeks in advance" conveys the demand for tattoos
- "people fall over themselves" hyperbole/word-choice suggests the demand for them

13. *A range of sensible answers are possible. Two marks for one of the following with a suitable comments.*

- Good conclusion as it returns to the idea that tattoos don't "stay that way" suggesting there are risks involved in the long-term

or/

- returns to the tattoo being "risky" as they might be "old-fashioned" one day

or/

- suggests that the "ink" under the skin will stay in demand unless it is linked to an illness

Regrets in Romania

In this passage the writer reflects on a family holiday to Romania. He describes how disappointed his family were, when they were unable to stay in the hotel they had paid for.

By 1980 my parents were tired of a Spain they had become too familiar with. They'd had enough of the sunburn, the sparse hotel rooms and vendors in the street selling us leather belts we did not need and sombreros we did not want. Spain had once been enough: a warm country where the sun came up in the morning and didn't go down until late. If there were 5 clouds in the sky, we didn't see them. But we'd had our last paella, our last evening of singing along to flamenco guitars. It was time for a change; time for some new place.

A travel agent some weeks later persuaded us that Romania was the "new Spain", a destination with advantages: your money would, thanks to low prices, last longer; the sea was like a warm bath to dip in; the hotel in the brochure looked lovely. Forget Spain and fly east, 10 was the recommendation they received. All of that, looking back now, turned out to be worse than nonsense.

In the middle of July, our plane left a grey, watery Glasgow and headed, like a migrating bird, into the clouds. The flight was a good one: no turbulence and after four and a half hours we glided onto a runway in Bucharest, Romania's capital city.

15 When the cabin door opened the air had that foreign, warm feel to it; a sensation you get when you are far from what you are used to. Coaches took us from the airport to our hotel. We saw workers in fields and little red-brick houses and dusty streets where people went about their normal day. Two hours later we pulled up in front of our hotel. It had palm trees and a swimming pool sunk into a huge, green front lawn. The lawn had tennis court stripes 20 and small lights dangled from the bushes. My mother, smiling like a member of cabin crew, said it was beautiful. We did not, however, get the chance to go in.

Within a few minutes a spokesman from the hotel boarded the bus, telling us through a crackling microphone that the hotel had been over-booked. Then he said we were not to worry as an alternative hotel had been found for us, not so far away. We would, he said, be 25 "well looked after".

Our new hotel was an old one. It *was* clean, but the rooms were drab and over rusty balcony railings outside our room, the view was unpleasant. Our accommodation had nothing but a burnt lawn in front of it. In fact, close to the lovely hotel we should have been in, were, at least, four drab hotels just like ours. We were beginning to understand the situation. At dinner 30 that night anyone we spoke to told us, with unsmiling faces, the same story. The palm-tree hotel, they too had learned, was "over-booked" and they, like us, were staying elsewhere and grumbling. "You save up all year to get away and then this happens!" This was the theme of the unhappy chatter around us.

There was nothing we could do. Being a long way from home reduces the volume of your 35 complaints. Dinner that night was mediocre. The soup was water-like and the "choice" of main course was limited. Drinks, if you wanted more than water, came to the table with prices as high as hotel rooftops. My parents were furious and the next day they marched forward to complain to the rep'. Her story was that "administrative errors" had led to the

good hotel being "over-booked". Angry by this time, they pointed out that everyone they met
40 was in the same situation. The "over-booking" had, it seemed, happened hundreds of times. Or could it be that the good hotel, palm trees, sea-blue swimming pool and all, simply appeared in the brochure to encourage the tourists? Once lured in, they would be placed in one of the older hotels that never appeared in the brochure. The rep' expressed her apologies but suggested that we made the best of it for the time being and then, after the holiday, took
45 our case to the office in Glasgow. An upgrade, at the moment, was out of the question as there was no place to upgrade to.

The mood in our camp was unpleasant: smiles changed to frowns; positive statements transformed to grumbles. Our hotel, we reminded ourselves, did not have a swimming pool! That did not matter apparently as we were permitted "access" to the pool at the good hotel;
50 that pool, however, was so crowded that actually swimming in it was impossible! Still, there was always the sea, that "warm bath", lapping on the sand. It was true; the sea was lovely and warm. The sand was the colour of a golden retriever. Things were looking up. The next morning, after an unpleasant breakfast, we sat on the sand and the swimming gear came out of our beach bags. Ten minutes of paddling about made you feel better: the water seemed
55 clear and inviting and lots of other people, swimming to either side of us, clearly enjoyed it too. This was the life! It was a facility that never closed and cost nothing.

Unfortunately, jelly fish enjoyed the water too. Floating like under-cooked fried eggs on the surface, you swam into them before you realised that your swim had become dangerous. They stung like wasps and so floating with them for "company" was unpleasant and
60 frightening. Some mornings the water was clear of them; at other times they took over and we "swimmers" were intimidated, limited paddlers, splashing about at the edge of the water.

This was a dark time. The wrong hotel, poor food, no chance of putting it right and now the sea was spoiled, polluted by strange, stinging creatures! We spent the last few days of the trip discontentedly wandering the streets of the nearby town. We bought a lunch from a half-
65 decent café to escape the hotel's food. The local shops around us sold trinkets and there were no prices on anything.

Buying things was complicated. The shop owner starting at a high price and, after about five minutes of ping-ponging figures, you came to an acceptable purchasing arrangement. My parents hated that. I would have hated it too only there was nothing I wanted to buy, unless I
70 wanted a bottle opener with "Rumania" on it, or a wooden footstool with the country's flag carved out of it.

The rest of the holiday slips from memory but I recall sitting happily on the plane a few days later, ready for our flight home. They end of a holiday is meant to be sad; we were all cheerful. For twenty minutes the plane did not move from the terminal. The pilot came on
75 the intercom: "Sorry for the delay, folks," he said, "but don't worry, we will soon be out of here!"

"That is the best news I have heard in two weeks," grumbled my mother.

We never went back to Rumania and even today, struggling to find good memories, it is only something we talk about regretfully.

James Getty

Questions – Regrets in Romania

1. Look at lines 1 – 3 and explain, using your **own words**, what the writer's parents had had enough of. **(2 marks)**
2. How does line 6 act as a **link** at this point in the passage? **(2 marks)**
3. How does the writer's **imagery**, lines 7 – 9, convince the reader that the sea was a good place to swim in? **(2 marks)**
4. Look at lines 12 – 14. How does the writer's **sentence structure** or **imagery** convince you that his flight was enjoyable? **(2 marks)**
5. Look at lines 15 – 18 and explain, using your **own words**, what the writer's first view of the country was like. **(2 marks)**
6. In lines 18 – 20 how do two examples of the writer's **word choice** convince you that the **first** hotel was attractive? **(2 marks)**
7. Look at lines 26 – 28 and, using your **own words**, explain two things he did not like about the hotel he was sent to. **(2 marks)**
8. How do two examples of the writer's **word choice**, lines 37 – 40, convey just how disappointed his parents were? **(2 marks)**
9. Look at lines 49 – 50. What is the author's tone in these lines and how is it created? **(2 marks)**
10. How do two examples of the writer's **word choice**, lines 50 – 56, convey the pleasure he feels about the sea at the start? **(4 marks)**
11. In lines 57 – 60 how does one example the writer's **imagery** convey his experience with the jelly fish? **(2 marks)**
12. Look at lines 62 – 66 and explain how the writer's **word choice** conveys his feelings about the holiday at this point. **(4 marks)**
13. Look at lines 72 – 79 and explain how **effective** you find this as a conclusion. You could examine **word choice** or **sentence structure** to help you in your answer. **(2 marks)**

30 Marks

Answers – Regrets in Romania

1. *Pupils must use their own words as far as possible. Complete quotations = zero marks. One mark for any of the following:*

    - Too familiar with Spain
    - Too much exposure to the sun
    - Basic accommodation
    - People always trying to get you to buy things

2. *Pupils need only identify how the sentence links forward OR backward for full marks. One mark for quotation and one mark for appropriate explanation.*

    - *"...time for a change"* returns to the idea of being tired of Spain; *"...time for some new place"* introduces their plans to go to Rumania.

3. *One mark for a quotation / identification of image and one mark for explanation.*

    - *"like a warm bath"* suggests the sea is pleasant, relaxing, comforting

4. *One mark for quotation / identification of techniques and one more for explanation.*

    Imagery:

    - *"like a migrating bird"* – the simile helps to suggest something purposeful, positive, even remarkable about the flight.

    Sentence Structure:

    - "The flight was a good one: no turbulence…" – the author uses a colon to create a pause and add additional information. This helps to emphasize the flight was enjoyable and trouble free.

5. *Pupils must use their own words as far as possible. Complete quotations = zero marks. One mark for of any of the following:*

    - People worked as farmers
    - The places they lived in were small
    - The streets were not clean

6. *One mark for quotation and one mark for appropriate explanation.*

- *"palm trees"* suggests it was exotic, elaborate gardens
- *"swimming pool"* suggests good facilities
- *"...huge green front lawn"* suggests it was attractive
- *"...tennis court stripes"* suggests a well maintained garden
- *"...lights dangled from the bushes"* suggests attractive garden

7. *Pupils must use their own words as far as possible. Complete quotations = zero marks. One mark for of any of the following:*

- Plain rooms
- Old fittings
- Distasteful things to look out at
- The grass was all destroyed by sun and lack of water

8. *One mark for quotation and one mark for appropriate explanation.* Any two from:

- *"...parents were furious"* suggests deep anger
- *"...marched forward to complain"* suggests a military-style approach
- *" Angry by this time..."* suggests they are not at all happy

9. *One mark for identification of tone. One mark for how the tone is created.*

The author's tone is ironic.
"access" – the quotation marks around this word change its meaning. The author is implying that they were, in fact, hardly able to swim in the pool at all.

10. *One mark for quotation and one mark for appropriate explanation.*

- *" warm bath"* – suggests a very pleasant experience
- *"..lovely and warm"* – suggests how pleasant the water was
- *" sand...colour of a golden retriever"* – suggests pleasant colour
- *"...the water seemed clear and inviting"* – suggests something pleasant
- *"...never closed"* suggests open access
- *"...cost nothing"* – suggests there is no price for access

11. *One mark for a quotation / identification of image and one mark for explanation.*

- *"Floating like under-cooked fried eggs..."* – suggests they were unpleasant and unattractive, possibly harmful

- *"...stung like wasps"* – *suggests* the stings were harmful and unpleasant and they can cause injury / illness

12. *One mark for quotation and one mark for appropriate explanation.*

- *"...dark time"* – suggests gloom and unhappiness
- *"wrong hotel"* – suggests inadequate accommodation
- *"poor food"* – suggests inadequate hospitality
- *" no chance of putting it right"* – suggests a hopelessness
- *"sea was spoiled"* – suggests his leisure area is ruined
- *"polluted by strange, stinging creatures"* – suggests he is frightened to swim with the jellyfish
- *"discontentedly wandering the streets"* – suggests he has nothing meaningful to do
- *"...escape the hotel's food"* – suggests he is unhappy with the hotel's offering

13. *Question should be marked on merit. One mark for a basic comment on ideas or techniques and two marks for a more in-depth analysis. Possible comments may include:*

Word choice:

- *"holiday slips from memory"* – suggests he wants to forget it
- *"sitting happily on the plane"* – suggests he wants to escape
- *"ready for our flight home"* – suggests he is eager to fly away
- *"meant to be sad; we...cheerful"* – contrast suggests happiness at leaving
- *"...something we talk about regretfully"* – suggests they do not want to bring it all up again/talk about it in a way that is full of bad memories

Sentence Structure

- Contrast of *"The end of the holiday is meant to be sad; we were cheerful"* – The sadness associated with holidays ending is not here. It is replaced with relief/high-spirits
- The parenthesis: *"struggling to find good memories"* – suggests that finding something pleasant to remember about the holiday is always difficult

About the authors:

James Getty and Tom Smart have over 25 years of teaching experience between them. Over the course of their careers, they have taught in numerous schools across Scotland, with James Getty marking for the SQA for several years. Tom and James also have an interest in journalism, contributing to a wide range of publications.

Both teachers think they might, after all this time, now have the skills necessary in order to read for understanding, analysis and evaluation. Their dream is that one day, mobile phones cease to work and, desperate for something resembling a computer screen, pupils have no choice but to read books. Until then, the authors hope this teaching resource is useful.

The authors can be contacted at: smartandgetty@hotmail.com

Acknowledgement of Artwork:

Many thanks to Caitlin Foulds for the lovely still life painting on the cover of this book.

Thank you as well to Holly Johnson for the cartoon of the authors above.

Printed in Poland
by Amazon Fulfillment
Poland Sp. z o.o., Wrocław